T0270603

"Jody Bahler's *The Homestead Cook* feels like a warm kitchen gathering, brimming with rich, simple recipes and heartfelt stories that feel like catching up with an old friend. Every page, beautifully captured, invites you to make everyday meals with a touch of homestyle charm and love."

SUZANNE WOODS FISHER
bestselling author of *A Healing Touch*

"Discover the timeless essence of family, food, and faith with *The Homestead Cook*. Jody Bahler's heartfelt recipes, steeped in tradition and crafted with love, offer a taste of cherished memories and the warmth of home. From appetizers to desserts, each dish invites you to embrace simplicity and celebrate the joy of gathering around the table. With its captivating stories and mouthwatering photography, this cookbook is more than just a collection of recipes—it's a culinary journey to be savored and shared for generations to come."

SUSAN HOUGELMAN
author of *Inside the Simple Life: Finding Inspiration among the Amish*

"Jody Bahler's cookbook is a trove of simple, traditional recipes and wonderful stories that add to the cookbook's charm. Surprise ingredients mean that you won't find tired, same-old recipes either. The Hard-Cooked Egg Casserole includes potato chips, the Herb Roasted Pork Loin is finished with a cilantro cream sauce, and the Snickers Apple Salad combines crunchy apples and caramelly candy bars—just three of the many wonderful recipes you can make to please your family with something special tonight. Delightful!"

GEORGIA VAROZZA
author of *The Homestead Canning Cookbook, The Homestead Sourdough Cookbook,* and *The Homestyle Amish Kitchen Cookbook*

"*The Homestead Cook* is a wonderful collection of recipes that have graced dinner tables and fellowship meals for decades. The rich and hearty recipes blend simple ingredients with good cooking and baking techniques to create dishes that delight."

MARSHALL V. KING
Midwestern food writer and author of *Disarmed: The Radical Life and Legacy of Michael "MJ" Sharp*

"Visually stunning, *The Homestead Cook* offers multigenerational recipes to satisfy your cravings for wholesome dishes while nourishing your soul with vignettes from the heartland."

SHERRY GORE
former editor-in-chief of *Cooking & Such Magazine* and author of *The Plain Choice* and *Me, Myself, and Pie*

"My personal passion for the beauty of the commonplace finds expression in the pages of this cookbook. Eating food is one of the most ordinary acts of being human, a ritual that becomes a feast when shared with loved ones. In this beautiful collection of recipes, Jody Bahler has taken the humblest of ingredients and invoked the taste of home itself."

RAE SLABACH
founder and owner of Daughters of Promise ministry

the
HOMESTEAD
COOK

JODY BAHLER

the HOMESTEAD COOK

EVERYDAY FAVORITES
TO CELEBRATE
RICH, SIMPLE LIVING

HERALD
PRESS

Harrisonburg, Virginia

Herald Press
PO Box 866, Harrisonburg, Virginia 22803
www.HeraldPress.com

Library of Congress Cataloging-in-Publication Data
Names: Bahler, Jody L., author.
Title: The homestead cook : everyday favorites to celebrate rich, simple
  living / Jody Bahler.
Description: Harrisonburg, Virginia : Herald Press, [2024] | Includes
  index.
Identifiers: LCCN 2024013186 (print) | LCCN 2024013187 (ebook) | ISBN
  9781513814520 (hardcover) | ISBN 9781513814537 (ebook)
Subjects: LCSH: Cooking, American. | BISAC: COOKING / General | COOKING /
  Comfort Food | LCGFT: Cookbooks.
Classification: LCC TX715 .B14826 2024 (print) | LCC TX715 (ebook) | DDC
  641.5973--dc23/eng/20240327
LC record available at https://lccn.loc.gov/2024013186
LC ebook record available at https://lccn.loc.gov/2024013187

THE HOMESTEAD COOK
© 2024 by Jody Bahler, released by Herald Press, Harrisonburg, Virginia 22803.
  800-245-7894. All rights reserved.
Library of Congress Control Number: 2024013186
International Standard Book Number: 978-1-5138-1452-0 (hardcover);
  978-1-5138-1453-7 (ebook)
Printed in China
Photography and food styling by Larissa Cottrell and Leandra Dotterer.
Family photography by Shelby Schambach Photography.

Scripture quotations are taken from the King James Version.

28 27 26 25 24   10 9 8 7 6 5 4 3 2 1

To our five girls: Amber, Larissa,
Leandra, Kenzie, and Erin

You were the inspiration behind this cookbook!

Many precious memories are deeply
woven throughout the recipes in this book,

far more than I could record, but they
are etched on the tables of our hearts.

I'll love you forever . . .

— Mom

CONTENTS

INTRODUCTION

I was raised on a dairy farm near the Flint Hills of Kansas—a simple life filled with dirt roads, faith, and family that I dearly cherish. Fast-forward several years: I married Mike, a handsome farmer from midwestern Indiana, and we moved onto his family's hundred-year-old farmstead. Within the next ten years we had five daughters together and found ourselves knee-deep in child-rearing. As a stay-at-home mom, I passed my time preparing food for my family, and I began to really enjoy experimenting and learning. I pored through recipe books, tweaking traditional recipes and coming up with new ideas of my own. I saw how food had the ability to light up the faces of my family, how it caused conversation to linger around the dinner table with each bite taken. I loved the excitement on my children's faces when I pulled a fresh dessert out of the oven after our meal or delighted them with a favorite after-school snack. This taught me that cooking good food doesn't have to be complicated or overwhelming. God uses food powerfully to bring people together, be it a family around a dinner table, a church family around a potluck, or friends at a fun gathering. So many cherished memories revolve around food—whether it is the taffy pull we remember from our childhood or our grandmother's homemade noodles. These familiar favorites bring a smile to our faces and comfort our souls.

As my interest in the kitchen grew, I took on some catering jobs for close friends. In 2010, after prayerful consideration and with a dream in our hearts, we opened The Homestead—a specialty home-style store offering bulk foods, a deli, a gift shop, baked treats, and convenient frozen entrees—in our local community. The Homestead has taken many turns over the past decade, but our mission has stayed the same: to serve our community with warm hospitality and delicious food.

Today, Mike and I are officially empty-nesters, and our five girls are starting families of their own. Sharing conversation and laughter around good food is always a highlight when we're together—I suspect it is for your family, too. Our longtime favorite recipes have been scattered in my kitchen, with hand-scribbled annotations and tweaks awaiting formal organization. Publishing a cookbook from a curated collection of these favorites has been a dream of mine—to include recipes from both the early days on the farm and from customer favorites we now serve at The Homestead (those recipes are marked with our logo).

This cookbook is a tribute to the deeply rooted heritage with which we have been blessed—a heritage full of faith in God, of beautiful relationships, and of living a simple life on a rural farmstead. It's a collection of traditional dishes meant to celebrate rich, simple living. As you step into these pages, I hope your senses come alive as you imagine the warm aromas, relate to the stories, and enjoy the beautiful photos. It is my prayer that *The Homestead Cook* becomes a keepsake in your family for years to come. With each recipe served, may you especially cherish the time that is spent with one another.

"The LORD is my rock, and my fortress, and my deliverer; my God, my strength, in whom I will trust" (Psalm 18:2).

— *Jody*

the fruit of
the Spirit is
love, joy, peace,
longsuffering,
gentleness,
goodness,
faith, meekness,
Temperance

GALATIANS 5:22-23

APPETIZERS AND BEVERAGES

Family gatherings just are not the same without tables laden with snacks to munch on!

FROZEN CAPPUCCINOS

Yields 24 (9-ounce) cups

This is a super easy way to enjoy a fancy frozen coffee drink whenever the urge hits. In their younger years, my girls made these often and kept them handy in the freezer for an after-school snack or as a treat after a hot summer day of work. We've served them for many luncheons and bridal showers, and they are always a hit. I still like to keep them in the freezer for when the girls and their families visit!

1. In a large bowl, whisk together the hot water, instant coffee, and sugar until dissolved.

2. Whisk in the coffee creamer, milk, and vanilla. Put the mixture into a large pitcher (for ease of pouring) and fill 24 clear plastic 9-ounce cups. Freeze on a large tray.

3. To serve, remove cups from the freezer and let them stand at room temperature for about 45 minutes. (If you just can't wait to dive in, pop them in the microwave on defrost for just a bit until you are able to chop the cappuccino into a slushy frozen consistency.) Top with a dollop of sweetened whipped cream or aerosol whip and sprinkle with chocolate sprinkles. Enjoy!

6 cups hot water

6 tablespoons instant coffee

2 cups sugar

4 cups hazelnut-flavored liquid coffee creamer (or desired flavor)

8 cups milk (2% or whole)

5 teaspoons vanilla extract

PIÑA COLADA SLUSH

Serves 12

We never tire of this refreshing slush drink. We even served it at two of our girls' wedding receptions. It can be made ahead and enjoyed later by guests, or you can dip into it for a serving here and there.

3 (6-ounce) cans pineapple juice (shake well)

1 (10-ounce) can frozen Bacardi Mixers Piña Colada juice concentrate, thawed*

1 (0.14-ounce) packet Crystal Light Lemonade powdered drink mix

2 cups cold water

1 tablespoon lime juice (shake well if using bottled concentrate)

⅓ cup sugar

1 (2-liter) bottle lemon-lime flavored carbonated beverage or ginger ale

Maraschino cherries, for garnish

Fresh pineapple wedges, for garnish

1. Whisk together the pineapple juice, piña colada concentrate, lemonade mix, water, lime juice, and sugar in a large container (I like to use an ice cream bucket). Cover and freeze for at least 24 hours.

2. When you are almost ready to serve, set the frozen bucket out on the counter for 45 to 60 minutes, then chop the mixture up. (I like to use my Pampered Chef chopper.) Mix the slush with equal parts carbonated beverage (you won't necessarily use the full bottle).

3. For a fancy presentation, top each slush cup with a long-stemmed maraschino cherry and a fresh pineapple wedge, if desired.

* *Note:* Not all grocery stores carry the frozen Bacardi Mixers Piña Colada juice concentrate. You can substitute 1½ cups pineapple juice concentrate plus 1 teaspoon coconut extract.

TROPICAL PUNCH

Serves 12

When the sun is hot and you need a good thirst-quencher, this slushy beverage with a twist of banana is refreshing. It can also be served as a slushy fruit cup side dish with a meal. If served as a side, I like to add some additional fruit, such as diced fresh strawberries, fresh blueberries, and mandarin oranges (drain if using canned fruit). This makes a delightfully refreshing addition to any meal. Try serving this alongside a cold taco salad on a hot summer day.

1. Bring the sugar and water to a rolling boil on the stove, then remove from heat, add the pineapple juice, orange juice, lemon juice, and bananas, and stir together well. Freeze in a large container (I like to use an ice cream bucket) for at least 24 hours.

2. When you are almost ready to serve, set the frozen bucket out on the counter for 45 to 60 minutes, then chop up the mixture. (A large spoon or a hand chopper work well; I like to use a Pampered Chef chopper.) Mix the slush with equal parts carbonated beverage (you won't necessarily use the full bottle). If desired, garnish with fresh fruit such as pineapple wedges or cherries.

1 cup sugar

2 cups water

2⅔ cups pineapple juice

1⅔ cups orange juice

4 teaspoons lemon juice

2 large ripe bananas, smashed with a fork

1 (2-liter) bottle lemon-lime flavored carbonated beverage or ginger ale

STRAWBERRY SMOOTHIE

Serves 4 to 6

There are some favorite handwritten recipes that continue to hang on the inside of my cupboard door at home, and this is one of them. This simple, delicious recipe was shared with me by my sister-in-law, Heidi. Back in the day when we were each raising our girls, they often got together to whip up this delicious smoothie. One sip of this will take you back to the berry patch on the farm!

1 cup milk

1 cup ice cubes

1 cup sugar

2 cups frozen whole strawberries

1 tablespoon vanilla extract

1. Pour all the ingredients into a blender. (It seems to work best if you put the milk in first.) Pulse and blend together until you achieve a smooth consistency. Pour into cups and enjoy immediately!

CARAMEL APPLE DIP

Serves 10 to 12

When September returns, so does this recipe! Slices of crisp apples—ripe from the tree—make a delicious snack to accompany a meal or to send with my husband Mike as he spends long days in the field. We also love to dip pretzel sticks in this sweet dip. There is something about the sweet/salty combination that just keeps you dipping for more!

1. Gently cook all the ingredients *except* the vanilla together on the stove over medium heat, stirring constantly for 5 minutes. Do not let it boil.

2. After 5 minutes, remove from heat and gently stir in the vanilla. Allow the dip to cool at room temperature for at least 30 minutes before serving. Refrigerate any leftover dip.

1 (14-ounce) can sweetened condensed milk

¾ cup packed brown sugar

½ cup (1 stick) butter, at room temperature

½ cup light corn syrup

Dash salt

¼ teaspoon vanilla extract

FRESH GARDEN SALSA

Serves 6 to 8

I don't make this salsa frequently, but it's hard to resist when sun-ripened Romas are loaded in the garden! Dipping into this cold salsa with crunchy chips on a hot summer day could well be considered a meal.

5 cups diced garden-fresh Roma tomatoes

½ cup finely chopped red onion

½ cup finely chopped green bell pepper

1 jalapeño pepper, seeds and membrane removed and finely chopped

1 teaspoon freshly chopped garlic

¼ to ½ cup freshly chopped cilantro

1 (15-ounce) can black beans, rinsed and drained

1 tablespoon olive oil

1 tablespoon white vinegar

1 teaspoon lemon juice

1½ teaspoons salt

1 teaspoon ground cumin

1 teaspoon sugar

1 teaspoon Crystal Light lemonade powdered drink mix*

½ teaspoon black pepper

1. Combine all the ingredients in a large bowl and refrigerate for at least 2 hours. Serve with your favorite tortilla chips. This salsa will keep for up to 1 week in the refrigerator, but I can guarantee that it will disappear before then!

* If you do not have powdered drink mix on hand, you may substitute up to 1 teaspoon additional lemon juice.

GRANDMA ISCH'S NACHO CHEESE DIP

Serves 10 to 12

My mom (the girls' grandma Isch) makes the best nacho cheese dip! She has served this to guests as an evening snack for as long as I can remember, and when the cousins are all together having a great time, this dip hits the spot. It whips up easily and freezes well.

1. Cut the cheese spread into small pieces and place in a microwave-safe bowl. Add salsa and cooked ground beef. Heat in the microwave, stirring often, until all contents are hot and melted together. Serve with tortilla chips.

This cheese dip can be made ahead and frozen. Once heated, it can also be kept warm in a small slow cooker.

2 pounds process cheese spread (I prefer Velveeta)

24 ounces mild chunky salsa (or medium/ hot if you prefer)

1 pound ground beef, cooked and drained and seasoned with salt and pepper

SMOKED CREAM CHEESE

Serves 4 to 6

This is my new favorite go-to appetizer. When the family comes home for Christmas, we let this smoke on our pellet smoker grill while we enjoy games around the table. It is effortless to make, and the finished product is amazing.

1 (8-ounce) block cream cheese (do not substitute low-fat cream cheese)

2 teaspoons packed brown sugar

1 teaspoon garlic powder

1 teaspoon onion powder

½ teaspoon paprika

½ teaspoon black pepper

1. Preheat the pellet smoker grill to 225°F.* With a sharp knife, score the top of the cream cheese in a crisscross pattern about halfway through the block.

2. In a bowl, stir together the brown sugar, garlic powder, onion powder, paprika, and pepper. Coat the top and sides of the scored cream cheese with this dry rub. Place the rubbed cream cheese in a small cast iron skillet or oven-safe pan.

3. Place the skillet, uncovered, on the grill and smoke at 225°F for 2 hours. Do not touch or stir. After 2 hours, remove from the grill. Serve as a warm appetizer with your favorite crackers.

Bahler family favorite: We like to drizzle ¼ cup Captain Rodney's Boucan Pepper Glaze over the block of seasoned, smoked cream cheese. It gives it just a hint of sweetness! (This glaze is available for purchase at The Homestead.)

* If you do not have a pellet smoker grill, you can bake this in the oven for similar results. The temperature and cooking time are the same.

GUACAMOLE

Serves 2 to 4

Guacamole doesn't keep very long, so a small batch is best. This freshly made snack is a favorite go-to, especially in the summer.

1. Stir all the ingredients together, mixing well. Add additional lime juice or salt for taste, if desired. Serve with your favorite tortilla chips, or set this on the table the next time you serve a Mexican dish. Try it with Chicken Tacos (p. 214).

2 ripe avocados, mashed with a fork

¼ cup finely chopped red onion

2 tablespoons finely chopped fresh cilantro

½ lime, squeezed and juiced*

Sea salt and black pepper, to taste

⅛ teaspoon garlic powder

* ***Tip:*** Roll your lime on the counter, applying pressure with your hands, before cutting and squeezing it. This loosens everything up inside and makes it so much easier to squeeze!

this is my commandment, that ye love one another, as I have loved you.

JOHN 15:12

CARAMEL CORN PUFFS

Serves 10 to 12

When I was a young girl and my family visited my grandpa and grandma Hartter, one of the highlights was always the many aunts, uncles, and cousins who gathered in their home for snacks after church. Grandma always had the best snacks, and this recipe is one that I will always fondly remember.

3 (5.5-ounce) bags, or about 1½ (11-ounce) bags Mikesell's Original Puffcorn*

1 cup (2 sticks) butter

1 cup packed brown sugar

½ cup light corn syrup

1 teaspoon baking soda

1. Preheat the oven to 250°F. Divide the puffcorn into two large mixing bowls and set aside.

2. In a large pot on the stove, combine the butter, brown sugar, and corn syrup. Heat and stir with a flat-bottomed spatula over medium heat. When the mixture just begins to reach a low bubble, set the timer for 2 minutes and continue to cook, stirring constantly. After 2 minutes, remove from heat and whisk in the baking soda. It will foam slightly, but this is normal.

3. Pour the mixture evenly over the bowls of puffcorn and stir well to coat. Spread out the coated puffcorn on a large, lightly greased baking sheet.

4. Bake at 250°F for 20 minutes. Let cool, then scrape up off the pan and store in a sealed container to keep it fresh. This will not last long!

* Mikesell's Original Puffcorn can be a little challenging to find in some grocery stores. It can also be purchased from online retailers.

PUPPY CHOW

Serves 12

An oldie but a goodie. This classic was one of the first treats that our girls learned to make. They made it often, and it is always enjoyed by everyone.

1. Dump the box of cereal into a large bowl. Set it aside. Melt the butter, chocolate chips, and peanut butter together in the microwave. Stir until melted and smooth. Pour the melted peanut butter and chocolate mixture over the dry cereal. Stir together until well coated.

2. Pour the chocolate-coated cereal into a large brown paper bag and add the powdered sugar. Roll the bag down tightly and shake well in all directions to coat the cereal with powdered sugar. Pour the coated cereal into a large bowl and dig in!

1 (12-ounce) box crisp rice cereal squares

½ cup (1 stick) butter

2 cups milk chocolate chips

1 cup smooth peanut butter

4 cups powdered sugar

PEANUT BUTTER
POWER BALLS

Yields 2 dozen balls

If you need a quick protein snack, this is it! These were a frequently requested snack when the girls planned weekend road trips with friends, and they usually left with a full container tucked under the seat. These are a popular Homestead customer favorite.

1 cup creamy peanut butter

¾ cup honey

2½ cups quick-cooking oats

¾ cup shredded coconut, toasted

¾ cup mini peanut butter chips

¾ cup mini semi-sweet chocolate chips

1. Whip the peanut butter and honey together. Add the remaining ingredients, mixing well. (Sometimes I prefer to use clean hands to mix, as it is easier to get everything stirred into this sticky dough.)

2. Divide the dough into 24 portions, shape, and round into smooth balls.

3. Store in the refrigerator, or freeze to enjoy later!

JALAPEÑO POPPERS

Yields 20 poppers

I'm not a big jalapeño fan, but when they are prepared this way I love them! Loaded with all the good stuff, they make a nice complement to any gathering, and there are never any left over.

1. Preheat the oven to 350°F. Cut peppers in half lengthwise. Remove the seeds, stems, and center membranes. (*Tip:* Cutting and seeding jalapeños submerged in a sink of cold water decreases the potential eye sting.)

2. Dry the washed peppers on a clean towel. Put the softened cream cheese in a piping bag for frosting (no tip needed) and pipe cream cheese into each pepper half. This is a mess-free way to fill peppers! Stretch a half-slice of raw bacon around each pepper half, wrapping tightly. Secure with a wooden pick, if desired. Place stuffed, wrapped poppers on a lightly greased baking sheet. Bake at 350°F for 40 to 45 minutes, or until the bacon is crispy.

10 large jalapeño peppers

6 ounces cream cheese, softened

10 bacon slices, cut in half lengthwise

STUFFED MUSHROOMS

Serves 20 to 24

This will forever be one of my husband Mike's favorite appetizers, and these savory stuffed mushrooms are often found on our Christmas dinner table. Mushrooms typically do not thrill me, but I'll admit, I usually reach for a second!

2 pounds large fresh white mushrooms, washed and dried

¼ cup (½ stick) butter

½ cup chopped white or yellow onion

½ cup plain fine breadcrumbs

1 cup finely shredded cheddar cheese

1 (8-ounce) package cream cheese, at room temperature

¾ cup fried bacon pieces

½ cup grated Parmesan cheese

½ cup mayonnaise

1 tablespoon dry Italian dressing mix (I prefer Good Seasons Italian Dressing mix)

1. Preheat the oven to 350°F.

2. Using a gentle twist and tug with your hands, break the stems off the clean mushrooms. Finely chop the stems and set aside in a bowl. Place the whole mushroom tops, underside up, on a lightly greased baking sheet.

3. Cook and stir the butter, onion, and chopped mushroom stems over medium heat for about 2 minutes, stirring constantly. Remove from heat and add the breadcrumbs and cheddar cheese. Stir together lightly and set aside.

4. In a separate bowl, mix together the cream cheese, bacon pieces, Parmesan cheese, mayonnaise, and dry dressing mix.

5. Combine the mushroom and cream cheese mixtures. Place the mushroom filling into a piping bag (do not use a tip). Pipe the filling into each mushroom top, overstuffing to maximize the flavor.

6. Bake, uncovered, at 350°F for 20 to 25 minutes, or until heated through.

Note: Extra filling can be stored in the refrigerator for up to 2 days and used to fill more mushrooms.

SWEET DILL PICKLES

Serves 10 to 12

Sweet dill pickles add a perfect crunch to any relish tray. They are also a fun snack to have handy when you need something cold and crunchy. I can guarantee that these will be sure to satisfy.

1. Drain the pickle jar and cut the baby pickles into chunky bite-size pieces. Place the pickle pieces back in the jar. Set aside.

2. On the stovetop, gently heat the sugar and white vinegar over medium heat until the sugar is completely dissolved, about 10 minutes. Stir often. Remove the hot mixture from the heat and set aside to cool completely.

3. When the syrup is cool, carefully pour this mixture over the pickles. Replace the cap and tighten. Turn the jar right side up, then upside down, alternating this every 30 minutes for the first 2 hours, then turn in the evening and in the morning for an additional 2 days.

4. After this period of turning, store pickles in the refrigerator.

1 (46-ounce) jar kosher baby dill whole pickles

3 cups sugar

1 cup white vinegar

VEGGIE PIZZA

Serves 16

It is a tradition of our church denomination to have a morning service followed by a light lunch and an hour of fellowship before gathering in the sanctuary for a second service. This recipe is often made and served for church lunch, and it disappears quickly.

2 (8-ounce) tubes crescent roll dough

12 ounces cream cheese, softened

¾ cup sour cream

1 teaspoon dill weed

1 teaspoon salt

½ teaspoon pepper

¼ teaspoon garlic powder

About 3¾ cups fresh vegetables, such as
    1 cup diced Roma tomatoes
    ¾ cup finely chopped bell peppers (seeds and membranes removed)
    ½ cup finely chopped broccoli
    ½ cup finely chopped cauliflower
    ½ cup finely shredded carrots
    ¼ cup finely chopped red onion
    ¼ cup finely shredded radish

1½ cups finely shredded sharp cheddar cheese, for topping (optional)

1. Preheat the oven to 375°F.

2. Unroll the crescent roll dough and press into a lightly greased 15 x 10-inch jelly roll pan. Seal the seams and press partway up the sides. Refrigerate the dough for 5 to 10 minutes before baking. Bake at 375°F for 15 to 20 minutes, or until lightly golden. Allow the crust to cool completely.

3. Beat the softened cream cheese and sour cream together with the dill weed, salt, pepper, and garlic powder. Once the crust is completely cooled, spread the cream cheese mixture over the crust. Top the pizza with the chopped fresh vegetables and lightly press them into the cream cheese layer. Serve immediately, or cover with plastic wrap and refrigerate for up to 24 hours.

4. Just before serving, I like to sprinkle finely shredded sharp cheddar cheese over top.

BREAKFAST DISHES

Now that the girls are grown, we don't sit down for morning breakfast anymore, but we have fond memories of eating breakfast around the table on those busy school mornings. Since Mike's favorite meal is breakfast, we do occasionally enjoy it on a cold winter evening. And we have started the tradition of gathering in our home with our girls and their families for breakfast around the table on the first Sunday morning of every month. I enjoy cooking for everyone, and it gives the girls a meal off. It is a blessing to be together before we all head to church.

DAD'S EGG AND TOAST

Serves 1

Mike is a hardworking hog and grain farmer, a husband and father whom we all adore, a handyman . . . a "can fix anything" kind of guy, but it's rare to find him in the kitchen fixing food. This is one dish that he occasionally made for the girls on school mornings. It was a treat when Dad made them breakfast! Maybe it was because they knew cooking wasn't really his thing, but for whatever reason, this recipe holds a special place in their hearts. It was always made with love, and they knew it.

1 egg

1 slice buttered toast

Salt and pepper

1. Place the egg in a pot and cover with water. Bring to a boil and boil for 5 minutes, then immediately remove the egg from the boiling water. Crack it hard with a table knife to split the shell in half. Using a spoon, scoop the egg out of the shell and spread it onto the buttered toast. The egg should be slightly hard around the edges and runny in the middle.

2. For the ultimate experience, cut the toast and egg into small squares, sprinkle with salt and pepper, and enjoy!

GRANDMA BAHLER'S BREAKFAST ENGLISH MUFFINS

Serves 8 to 12

Grandma Bahler will forever be remembered by this delicious breakfast treat! When the girls stayed overnight, they always knew this would be served for breakfast, and they so looked forward to it.

1. Turn the broiler on low. Halve the English muffins, then mix the remaining ingredients together and spread on English muffin halves like you would a sandwich spread.

2. Place the English muffin halves on a baking sheet. Broil for 5 minutes, or until the tops are bubbling and lightly golden. Watch closely so they don't burn.

3. Let cool for 5 minutes before serving.

1 (6-count) package English muffins

2 cups shredded cheddar cheese

1 cup chopped shaved ham (may substitute fried bacon, cooked ground sausage, or a combination)

1 cup mayonnaise

½ cup fried bacon pieces

BACON AND EGG SALAD

Serves 6 to 8

I created this recipe by adding a little of this and a little of that to come up with this meaty version of egg salad. It is delicious served on a toasted croissant or toasted homemade Cinnamon Swirl Bread (p. 168). We like to serve it in our salad bar at The Homestead.

2 ounces cream cheese, softened

¼ cup mayonnaise

¼ cup whipped salad dressing (such as Miracle Whip)

6 tablespoons sour cream

2 tablespoons finely chopped yellow onion

½ teaspoon sugar

½ teaspoon parsley flakes

¼ teaspoon dried chives

¼ teaspoon garlic powder

¼ teaspoon salt

⅛ teaspoon pepper

½ teaspoon sweet pickle juice

¾ cup fried bacon pieces (sautéed lightly in 1 tablespoon butter)

6 hard-cooked eggs, diced

1. Beat together the cream cheese, mayonnaise, whipped salad dressing, and sour cream until smooth. Then add the onion, sugar, parsley flakes, chives, garlic powder, salt, pepper, and sweet pickle juice. Mix well. Stir in the fried bacon pieces and hard-cooked eggs. Keep refrigerated.

BLUEBERRY FRENCH TOAST CASSEROLE

Serves 10 to 12

I would classify this as comfort food at its finest. Pair this with grilled sausage links, fresh fruit, and a steamy cup of coffee, and it will warmly satisfy your morning. This casserole is refrigerated overnight before baking the next morning. It can also be frozen and pulled out later to thaw, bake, and serve.

1. Cut the bread into ½-inch cubes and place half of them in a greased 13 x 9-inch baking pan, covering the bottom as best as you can. Cut the cream cheese into ½-inch cubes and place them evenly over the bread. Top with evenly distributed fresh blueberries, followed by the remaining cubes of bread.

2. In a large bowl, beat together the eggs, milk, syrup, and vanilla. When well mixed, carefully pour this evenly over the bread mixture in the pan. Cover tightly with plastic wrap and refrigerate overnight or at least 8 hours.

3. *To make streusel topping:* In a separate bowl, mix together the melted butter, flour, brown sugar, and cinnamon. Cover and let it stand on the counter overnight or at least 8 hours.

4. Remove the casserole from the refrigerator 30 to 60 minutes before baking. Preheat the oven to 350°F. Cover pan lightly with aluminum foil and bake at 350°F for 30 minutes. Uncover and sprinkle with streusel topping. Bake an additional 25 to 30 minutes, or until the casserole is puffed, lightly golden, and center is set. Let rest 10 minutes before serving. Enjoy drizzled with additional Maple Pancake Syrup.

1½-pound loaf French bread or any other white bread

2 (8-ounce) packages cream cheese, softened

1¼ cups fresh blueberries

12 eggs

2 cups milk

⅓ cup Maple Pancake Syrup (p. 70) plus additional for serving

1 teaspoon vanilla extract

Streusel topping

¼ cup (½ stick) butter, melted

½ cup flour

6 tablespoons packed brown sugar

½ teaspoon ground cinnamon

o taste and
see that the
Lord is good:
blessed is the
man that
trusteth
in him.

PSALM 34:8

BREAKFAST CASSEROLE

Serves 10 to 12

We love the convenience of a good, hearty breakfast casserole. This one fills the bill. It's so simple yet always hits the spot. It can also be made ahead and refrigerated overnight or frozen for longer-term storage.

¾ **pound process cheese spread, sliced**

1½ **pounds country seasoned sausage, cooked, drained, and crumbled**

3 **cups shredded cheddar cheese**

18 **eggs**

2¼ **cups milk**

1¼ **teaspoons salt**

½ **teaspoon pepper**

¼ **teaspoon garlic powder**

Dried parsley, for topping

1. Preheat the oven to 350°F (skip this step for now if you will be refrigerating or freezing to bake and serve later). Line the bottom of a greased 13 x 9-inch baking pan with slices of process cheese spread. Sprinkle cooked sausage evenly over the cheese. Spread shredded cheddar cheese over all.

2. In a bowl, beat together the eggs, milk, salt, pepper, and garlic powder. Carefully pour the egg mixture over the casserole. Sprinkle with dried parsley.

3. Bake immediately, or cover and refrigerate to bake and serve the next day. Bake, uncovered, at 350°F for 45 to 60 minutes, or until the center is cooked and set. Remove from the oven and let it rest for 10 minutes before slicing and serving.

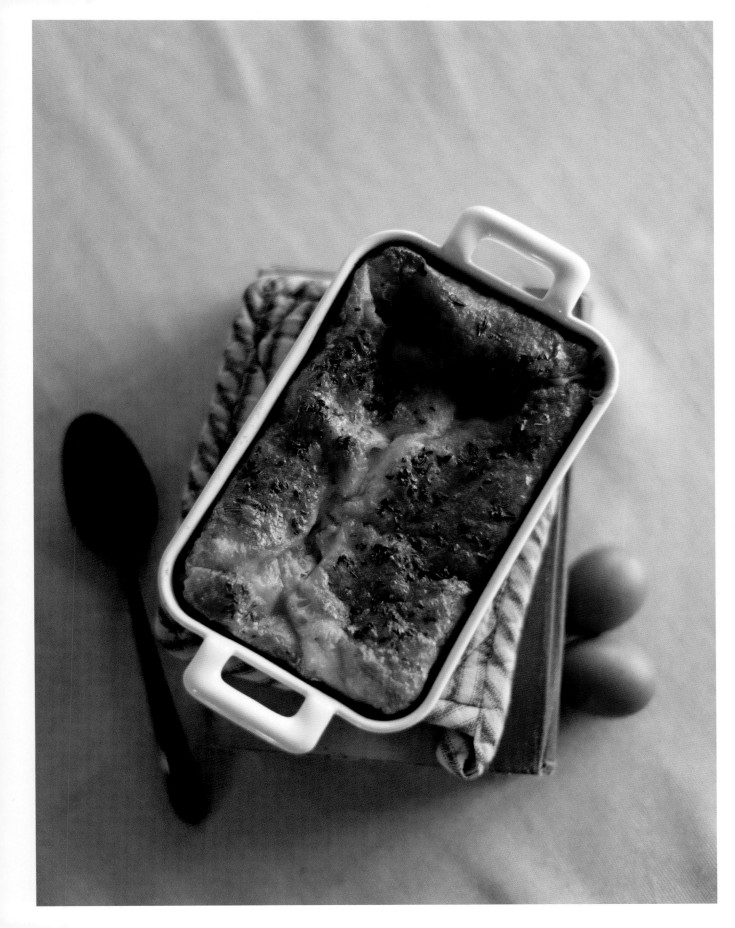

HARD-COOKED EGG CASSEROLE

Serves 8 to 10

Time and time again this casserole makes it to the breakfast table. It's always everyone's first choice! If you need a shortcut when making this recipe, you can purchase hard-cooked eggs at most larger grocery stores. To mix it up, my sister-in-law Liz has used a variety of flavored potato chips in this recipe instead of plain, with delicious results!

1. Preheat the oven to 350°F. On the stovetop, cook the onions in butter for a few minutes, stirring often. Stir in the flour. Add the milk and whisk well, continuing to whisk and stir until the mixture bubbles and thickens. Add cubed cheese spread, salt, pepper, and garlic powder. Stir until the cheese is melted and the sauce is smooth.

2. In a greased 13 x 9-inch pan, layer half the sliced hard-cooked eggs. Pour half the cheese sauce over top, then layer half the crushed potato chips and half the fried bacon pieces. Repeat the layers, ending with crushed potato chips and fried bacon pieces. Bake, uncovered, at 350°F for 25 to 35 minutes, or until the casserole is bubbling around the edges and the center is hot.

½ cup diced onion

6 tablespoons (¾ stick) butter

6 tablespoons flour

3 cups milk

¾ to 1 pound process cheese spread, cut into small cubes

2 teaspoons salt

1 teaspoon pepper

½ teaspoon garlic powder

12 hard-cooked eggs, thinly sliced (an egg slicer works best)

2½ cups crushed salted potato chips

1 pound bacon, fried and crumbled, or 1½ cups precooked bacon pieces

Tip: This casserole can be made a few days in advance and refrigerated, but it does not freeze well. The hard-cooked eggs can become rubbery if frozen.

SPINACH BACON QUICHE

Serves 6 to 8

Even those who look skeptically at spinach love this quiche. It is full of cheese and fried bacon, and when you pair this with my Flaky Pie Crust (p. 272), the combination is amazing! Larissa has used this quiche filling in individual wonton wrappers placed inside a muffin tin. They are delicious!

Filling

½ cup fried bacon pieces

1 (10-ounce) package frozen spinach, thawed and squeezed

2 tablespoons chopped green onion

2 cups shredded Monterey Jack cheese

½ cup shredded cheddar cheese

1½ cups milk

3 eggs, beaten

1 tablespoon flour

½ teaspoon Shipshewana Happy Salt or another seasoned salt

⅛ teaspoon garlic powder

1 (9-inch) unbaked pie shell (see recipe for Flaky Pie Crust, p. 272)

½ cup additional fried bacon pieces, for topping

1. Preheat the oven to 350°F. Stir the filling ingredients together and pour this mixture into the unbaked pie shell. It's okay if the filling is level with the crimp line—just be careful not to spill on the crimped edge if possible.

2. Sprinkle ½ cup additional fried bacon pieces on top of the quiche. Bake at 350°F for 1 hour or longer, until the center of the quiche is puffy and set.

3. Remove from the oven and let the quiche stand for 15 minutes before serving.

FOUR-CHEESE EGG BAKE

Serves 6 to 8

This is a great egg breakfast dish to serve alongside fried bacon or sausage links.

1. Preheat the oven to 350°F. In a large mixing bowl, beat together the eggs, milk, flour, baking powder, garlic powder, garlic salt, salt, and pepper. With a rubber spatula, stir in the melted butter, cottage cheese, cream cheese, and Monterey Jack and Colby cheeses. Carefully pour this mixture into a well-greased 13 x 9-inch baking dish. Cut thin slices of cold butter and dot it across the top of the casserole. Lightly sprinkle with additional garlic salt and parsley.

2. Bake, uncovered, at 350°F for 45 to 60 minutes, or until the center is set and the eggs are lightly golden. Let stand 10 minutes before slicing and serving.

6 eggs

1 cup milk

½ cup flour

1 teaspoon baking powder

½ teaspoon garlic powder

½ teaspoon garlic salt plus additional for sprinkling

⅛ teaspoon salt

⅛ teaspoon pepper

2 tablespoons (¼ stick) butter, melted

8 ounces cottage cheese (small curd 4% milkfat)

3 ounces cream cheese, cubed

8 ounces Monterey Jack cheese, shredded or cubed

8 ounces Colby cheese, shredded or cubed

¼ cup (½ stick) cold butter

Parsley flakes

FEATHER PANCAKES WITH MAPLE PANCAKE SYRUP

Serves 6 to 8

When I found this pancake recipe that I loved, I didn't look any further! I like them plain or with fresh blueberries sprinkled in. The girls always preferred them studded with milk chocolate chips.

1 cup flour

2 tablespoons baking powder

2 tablespoons sugar

½ teaspoon salt

1 egg, beaten

1 cup milk

2 tablespoons canola oil

Butter, for frying

Blueberries or chocolate chips (optional)

Maple Pancake Syrup

¼ cup granulated sugar

¼ cup packed brown sugar

¼ cup light corn syrup

¼ cup water

½ teaspoon maple extract

1. Mix together the flour, baking powder, sugar, and salt in a bowl. Add the egg, milk, and canola oil and beat until just blended. Let the batter rest for about 15 minutes. While the batter rests, preheat the griddle or skillet to medium heat.

2. Melt small pats of butter on the hot griddle or skillet and pour small circles (about ¼ cup) of batter over the melted butter. Spread the batter out a little. Let it fry on one side, then flip and fry on the other side.

3. If adding fresh blueberries or chocolate chips, drop these into the batter as soon as you spread it on the griddle. Serve with syrup.

4. *To make Maple Pancake Syrup:* Whisk together the granulated sugar, brown sugar, light corn syrup, and water in a small saucepan on low to medium heat until it starts to lightly bubble around the edges. Remove from heat and add the maple extract. Enjoy this syrup drizzled over the hot pancakes.

FRENCH TOAST WITH RASPBERRY SAUCE

Serves 6 to 8

There's something about sinking your teeth into a buttery, crispy slice of hot French toast that is so satisfying! When eating this dish, one of our sons-in-law once exclaimed, "It's like candy!" I often use store-bought plain French bread from the bakery department or make my own (see French Bread Loaves, p. 175).

1. Preheat a griddle or skillet to medium heat. Slice the French bread into ¾-inch slices and spread one side of each slice with a thick layer of softened butter. (It seems like so much butter, but really, this is what raises the bar.) Set the buttered slices aside.

2. In a medium-size bowl, beat together the eggs, milk, and vanilla. Submerge each buttered bread slice in the egg mixture, then fry (buttered side down) on the heated griddle or skillet for a couple of minutes until golden and crispy. Flip the slices and fry the other side. When both sides are golden and crispy, remove from heat and arrange on a serving platter. Sprinkle the hot, crispy toast with powdered sugar. Serve with prepared and slightly cooled Raspberry Sauce or with Maple Pancake Syrup (p. 70).

3. *To make Raspberry Sauce:* Whisk all the sauce ingredients together on the stovetop. Bring to a low bubble for 2 minutes. Remove from heat and allow to cool to lukewarm before serving over French toast. This sauce is also delicious cold!

1 (16-ounce) loaf French bread

¾ cup (1½ sticks) butter, softened

3 eggs

1½ cups milk

½ teaspoon vanilla extract

Powdered sugar, for topping

Raspberry Sauce

2 cups fresh raspberries, mashed

¼ cup raspberry jam

¼ cup sugar

1 tablespoon cornstarch or Thermflo

1 tablespoon raspberry flavored gelatin powder

½ cup cold water

SCHOOL MORNING PUFF PANCAKE

Serves 6 to 8

If you're in a hurry and need a quick breakfast, this would be a recipe to use. It's a little shocking the first time you pull the pancake out of the oven and see the puffy shape, but it soon settles down and can be sliced into nice squares. Sometimes I sprinkle the batter with a cinnamon-and-sugar mixture just before I pop it into the oven.

½ cup (1 stick) butter

6 eggs

1½ cups milk

1½ cups flour

¼ teaspoon salt

1. Preheat the oven to 425°F and melt butter in a 13 x 9-inch pan or a 12-inch cast iron skillet. (I like to stick the pan in the oven as it's heating to melt the butter.)

2. In a separate bowl, beat together the eggs, milk, flour, and salt. Pour this mixture into the pan of melted butter. Bake at 425°F for 20 to 25 minutes. It will be moderately golden, and butter may be pooled in the center of the puff pancake. This is the way it is supposed to look. Slice, and serve with Maple Pancake Syrup (p. 70).

SAUSAGE GRAVY AND FRESH BUTTERMILK BISCUITS

Serves 6 to 8

I like to make a few extra biscuits to also serve with butter and honey at the table, since Mike likes to finish a meal with something sweet. I have found that Grands! frozen biscuit pucks are delicious, or I make my own.

1. *To make Sausage Gravy:* On the stovetop, cook the sausage in a pan lightly greased with cooking spray. Crumble and drain the cooked sausage. Add the flour, stirring well. Gradually add milk, and continue to heat over medium heat, stirring constantly, until the gravy bubbles and thickens. Remove from heat. Whisk in the seasoned salt, garlic salt, pepper, and cheese spread. Stir until the cheese spread is melted. Serve over freshly baked, hot buttermilk biscuits.

2. *To make Fresh Buttermilk Biscuits:* Preheat the oven to 425°F. Whisk together the flour, baking powder, and salt, then cut in the cold butter with a pastry blender. Create a well in the center and add the buttermilk. Mix gently with a fork, just until combined.

3. Roll out the dough to ½ inch thickness and cut about 12 biscuits with a biscuit cutter. Place biscuits on a lightly greased baking sheet, sides touching. Bake at 425°F for 13 to 15 minutes, or until lightly golden. Enjoy hot biscuits!

Sausage Gravy

1 pound ground seasoned sausage

¼ cup flour

3 cups milk

½ teaspoon Shipshewana Happy Salt or another seasoned salt

¼ teaspoon garlic salt

¼ teaspoon pepper

⅓ cup cubed process cheese spread

Fresh Buttermilk Biscuits

2½ cups flour

1 tablespoon baking powder

1 teaspoon salt

½ cup (1 stick) cold butter, thinly sliced

1 cup cold buttermilk*

* If you do not have buttermilk, you can make a buttermilk substitute with milk and vinegar: Pour 1 tablespoon white vinegar into a small liquid measuring cup. Add milk to the 1-cup line. Stir gently, then let this mixture sit for 5 minutes as the milk "sours" and thickens.

SOUPS, SANDWICHES, SALADS, AND DRESSINGS

We love a steamy pot of soup on a cold winter day. Even better, soups are one of those things that almost seem to taste better reheated the second day. And who doesn't love a delicious salad to complement your soup or to enjoy as a side dish to any meal? Store-bought dressings just don't compare with fresh, homemade salad dressings. Plus, they're simple and they last for weeks in the refrigerator thanks to their vinegar and sugar content.

CHEESY BROCCOLI NOODLE SOUP

Serves 6 to 8

Years ago, we enjoyed dining at The Barn, a popular restaurant in Smithville, Ohio. They were known for their cheesy broccoli noodle soup. I loved it so much that I came home to experiment and ended up with my own version. We serve this popular soup to our Homestead customers. It is frequently requested by our son-in-law, Eli.

¼ cup chopped onion

2 tablespoons (¼ stick) butter

1 (8-ounce) package cream cheese, at room temperature, cut into cubes

2½ cups milk

1 teaspoon granulated chicken bouillon

¾ cup boiling water

1 (10.5-ounce) can cream of mushroom soup

10 ounces chopped frozen broccoli, cooked and drained

¾ cup cubed process cheese spread

½ teaspoon lemon juice

½ teaspoon salt

½ teaspoon pepper

½ cup uncooked thin egg noodles

1. Cook and stir the onion in the butter until tender, about 5 minutes. Add the softened cubes of cream cheese and milk. Stir continuously over low heat until the cream cheese completely melts. (It is helpful to use a wire whisk.) Dissolve the chicken bouillon in the boiling water and add to the creamy mixture. Add the cream of mushroom soup. Stir in the cooked, drained broccoli as well as the cubed process cheese spread, lemon juice, salt, and pepper.

2. Heat thoroughly over low-medium heat until the soup just starts to gently bubble around the edges. You don't want it to be a full-blown boil. When the soup is lightly bubbling around the edges, stir in the uncooked noodles. Let the soup simmer for 5 to 10 minutes, or until the noodles are tender.

3. If the soup seems too thick, add a little chicken broth or hot water until the desired thickness is reached.

LOADED BAKED POTATO SOUP

Serves 6 to 8

This soup is one of my favorites. Anytime you load a potato—in any form—with bacon, cheese, and onion, it will be delicious. This soup will warm you to your toes on a cold winter night.

1. Preheat the oven to 400°F.

2. Place cubed potatoes on a large rimmed baking sheet. Drizzle with olive oil and season with garlic salt and salt and pepper as desired. Toss with clean hands to coat the potatoes with the oil and seasonings. Roast, uncovered, at 400°F for 25 to 30 minutes, stirring partway through roasting. When the potatoes are roasted and tender, remove them from the oven and set them aside.

3. In a large microwave-safe bowl, combine the melted butter, milk, and flour, and heat in the microwave for approximately 10 minutes, stopping every minute to whisk until the mixture is heated and slightly thickened. Whisk in the 1½ teaspoons additional garlic salt, garlic powder, onion powder, pepper, and cubed cheese spread. Stir until smooth and the cheese spread is melted. Gently stir in the roasted potatoes.

4. Serve with fried bacon pieces, chopped green onion, and a sprinkling of shredded cheddar cheese for an amazing, filling bowl of soup.

2 pounds russet, red, or yellow potatoes, cleaned and cut into ¾-inch cubes (leave skins on)

¼ cup (or less) olive oil

Garlic salt

Salt and pepper

½ cup (1 stick) butter, melted

4 cups milk

½ cup flour

1½ teaspoons additional garlic salt

½ teaspoon garlic powder

⅛ teaspoon onion powder

⅛ teaspoon pepper

½ pound process cheese spread, cubed

Fried bacon pieces, for topping

Chopped green onions, for topping

Shredded cheddar cheese, for topping

SAUSAGE POTATO SOUP

Serves 8 to 10

Anything with sausage and potatoes is guaranteed to be flavorful, and this soup is no exception. I always made up this soup as I went along, but one day I decided to jot it down for my girls. Enjoy!

8 large russet potatoes, peeled and coarsely chopped

2 stalks celery, diced

1 cup matchstick carrots (available in the produce department)

2 pounds country sausage

½ cup diced onion

½ cup (1 stick) butter

½ cup flour

4 cups milk

1¼ teaspoons garlic salt

½ teaspoon garlic powder

¼ teaspoon pepper

1 pound process cheese spread, cubed

1. Combine the potatoes, celery, and carrots in a 6- to 8-quart stockpot. Cover with water (by about 1 inch), then cook over medium heat until potatoes are tender. Shut off the burner and set aside—do *not* drain. Using a potato masher, partially mash the mixture, leaving some chunks of potato (you'll want those in your soup).

2. Meanwhile, cook and brown the sausage with the onion. Drain well and set aside.

3. Make a cheese sauce by melting the butter and whisking in the flour, then the milk, garlic salt, garlic powder, and pepper. I like to cook this in the microwave, stopping every couple of minutes to whisk the mixture until it thickens slightly. When thickened, add the cubes of cheese spread, heating and stirring until melted and smooth. Add the cooked, drained sausage and the cheese sauce to the smashed potato mixture in the stockpot. Carefully stir all together using a rubber spatula. Heat gently to serve. If the soup is too thick, add a little water or milk to thin it down.

TORTELLINI SOUP

Serves 12 to 15

I once had tortellini to use up, so I created this hearty soup chock-full of beef, sausage, and cheese tortellini. Its creamy base is so comforting on a cold night. Light the fireplace and let this soup add to the warmth and coziness of the evening. This makes a large batch, so I like to freeze part of it to pull out another day. It's delightful served with garlic bread on the side.

1. Cook the beef, sausage, and onion together. Drain well. Put the drained meat into a large stockpot and add the remaining ingredients *except* the tortellini, sour cream, and mozzarella cheese. Simmer this mixture for about 20 minutes, then add the tortellini. Simmer an additional 20 minutes.

2. Remove from heat and stir in the sour cream until well blended. I like to serve it with shredded mozzarella cheese at the table.

1 pound ground beef

1 pound ground country sausage

1 cup diced onion

2 (10.5-ounce) cans tomato soup

1 (14.5-ounce) can fire-roasted diced tomatoes (do not drain)

1 (24-ounce) jar traditional pasta sauce (I prefer Prego brand or Botticelli Roasted Garlic Premium Pasta Sauce)

1 cup matchstick carrots (available in the produce department)

¼ cup packed brown sugar

4 tablespoons granulated beef bouillon

3 tablespoons dried parsley

1 teaspoon dried basil

1 teaspoon dried oregano

1 teaspoon garlic salt

8 cups hot water

20 ounces cheese tortellini

1 cup sour cream

Shredded mozzarella, for serving (optional)

HOMESTEAD CHILI

Serves 10 to 12

How can there be over one hundred different versions of chili? There really are! Everyone makes chili a little differently. This recipe was created when our daughter Larissa entered a chili cook-off contest while she was in high school. She came up with this recipe, and it won the grand prize. I made some minor adaptations and created Homestead Chili. It's still one of my favorite soups, especially when it is topped with sour cream, shredded cheddar cheese, and crushed nacho cheese Dorito chips at the table.

2 tablespoons canola oil

1 cup finely chopped onion

1 green bell pepper, finely diced

2 teaspoons minced fresh garlic

½ cup packed brown sugar

5 tablespoons plus 1 teaspoon ancho chili seasoning

1½ teaspoons Shipshewana Happy Salt or another seasoned salt

1 teaspoon dried oregano

2 pounds ground beef, cooked and drained

2 (16-ounce) cans petite diced tomatoes (do not drain)

1 (16-ounce) can mild chili beans, drained

1 (15.25-ounce) can black beans, rinsed and drained (I prefer to use only three-quarters of the can)

1 (16-ounce) can tomato puree

16 ounces tomato juice

⅔ cup water

1. In a large stockpot on the stove, cook the oil, onion, bell pepper, and garlic together for 10 minutes, stirring often. Add the brown sugar, chili seasoning, seasoned salt, and oregano, stirring well. Add the cooked and drained ground beef and the remaining ingredients. Stir gently and simmer on the stove for 20 to 30 minutes.

2. This soup almost tastes better the next day after it has cooled down and been reheated. This gives the flavors time to meld and soak into the meat and beans.

ITALIAN BEEF SANDWICH

Serves 6 to 8 (yields about 2 pounds finished product)

I love to make this ahead and freeze it for later. It's easy to pull out and thaw for sandwiches. Serve it on a salted pretzel bun with sliced Provolone cheese. The hot Italian beef melts the cheese, and it is just delightful!

1. Grease a large slow cooker with cooking spray, or easier yet, use a slow-cooker liner for easy cleanup (I still spray the liner). Place the chuck roast into the slow cooker with the pepperoncini, ½ cup of the pepperoncini juice, Italian dressing mix, gravy mix, salt, and pepper. Cover the slow cooker and heat on high for 10 to 12 hours. (Turn the heat down the last couple of hours.)

2. After 10 to 12 hours, shut off the slow cooker, remove the lid, and let it cool down for about 30 minutes. Discard any bone, gristle, or fat, then shred the meat and whole pepperoncini with a fork. (If the meat is cool enough, I find it easier to do this with clean hands. But do not let it cool down completely or refrigerate it before shredding.)

3. Drizzle in the remaining ½ cup pepperoncini juice and the Italian dressing and stir into the shredded beef mixture. Place the finished product in a lightly greased pan, or divide into several smaller pans for freezing for future meals.

4. At this point, the mixture can be frozen for future meals. If serving, cover the pan tightly with aluminum foil and heat at 350°F for 20 to 30 minutes, or until the shredded beef is heated through. Garnish with a few whole pepperoncini when serving, and include some sliced pepperoncini for individual sandwiches.

3 to 4 pounds chuck roast

8 whole mild pepperoncini plus additional for garnish

1 cup pepperoncini juice, divided

2 tablespoons dry Italian dressing mix (I prefer Good Seasons brand)

2 tablespoons dry brown gravy mix

½ teaspoon salt

⅛ teaspoon pepper

¼ cup Italian dressing (I prefer Kraft Zesty Italian Dressing)

Salted pretzel buns, for serving

Sliced provolone cheese, for serving

PHILLY CHEESESTEAK SANDWICH

Serves 4 to 6

If Mike had to choose one sandwich to live on, it would be this one. A tip: It is so much easier to slice the steak into thin strips when it is partially (mostly) frozen. The meat doesn't get smushed, and a sharp serrated knife will cut nice, even slices. I've also found it helpful to stand the partially (mostly) frozen steak on edge to cut it rather than laying it flat.

1 onion, thinly sliced

2 green bell peppers, thinly sliced

¼ cup (½ stick) butter

Garlic salt, as desired

3-pound flat iron steak (a sirloin cut also works well), cut into thin ¼-inch strips

4 teaspoons Worcestershire sauce

¼ teaspoon additional garlic salt

¼ teaspoon pepper

½ cup (1 stick) butter, at room temperature

1 teaspoon parsley flakes

¼ teaspoon dried dill weed

¼ teaspoon dried oregano

⅛ teaspoon garlic powder

4 to 6 sub buns

¼ pound sliced provolone cheese

Horseradish Sauce

2½ cups sour cream

½ cup prepared horseradish

¼ teaspoon Worcestershire sauce

2½ teaspoons coarsely ground pepper

1. Cook and stir the thinly sliced onions and bell peppers in the butter for just a couple of minutes until crisp-tender. Sprinkle with garlic salt. Remove vegetables from the skillet and set aside.

2. Place the thin-cut strips of steak in the skillet with the Worcestershire sauce, ¼ teaspoon additional garlic salt, and pepper. Cook the steak strips just until slightly browned, stirring often. Add the vegetables back in with the steak and continue to cook all together for a few minutes until the meat is no longer pink.

3. In a small bowl, mix the softened butter, parsley, dill weed, oregano, and garlic powder. Spread this herb butter on both sides of individual sub buns and toast them on a separate skillet. Assemble sandwiches piled with the beef mixture and slices of provolone cheese. Serve with Horseradish Sauce.

4. *To make Horseradish Sauce:* Stir all the sauce ingredients together. This is also delicious served with prime rib.

AUNT ILENE'S ITALIAN DRESSING

AUTHENTIC RECIPE
THE HOMESTEAD
FROM THE HOMESTEAD

Yields 3 cups

Aunt Ilene makes the best Italian dressing (pictured at left). It's been our family favorite for years. And it's the source of a good story.

Several years back we traveled to attend a church fellowship weekend in Kansas. We enjoyed a nice dinner on Saturday evening with over a hundred guests in attendance. Aunt Ilene was on the food committee serving the meal. I sat down to enjoy the meal and stuffed a forkful of salad in my mouth. I could hardly choke down the bland, tasteless wad that hit my palette. As hard as I tried, I could not finish the salad. Later, Aunt Ilene came up to ask me if I enjoyed the salad. Gulp. The group of hosts were the last ones to sit at the table. After Uncle Roger took one bite of salad, he leaned over to Aunt Ilene and asked, "What in the world is wrong with this dressing?" I can only imagine how the color must have drained from her face when she realized that she had grabbed the jar of peanut oil that she had recently used to fry apple fritters instead of the jar of her Italian dressing! We still laugh about this story—including Aunt Ilene!

1. Blend all the ingredients in the blender for 5 minutes. Store in the refrigerator.

1 cup canola oil

½ cup apple cider vinegar

1 cup sugar

2 tablespoons finely diced white onion

½ teaspoon onion salt

½ teaspoon garlic powder

½ teaspoon dry mustard

¼ teaspoon pepper

½ teaspoon salt

CREAMY ITALIAN DRESSING

Yields 2½ to 3 cups

Another delicious dressing.

1. Blend all the ingredients in the blender for 5 minutes. Store in the refrigerator.

1 cup canola oil

½ cup apple cider vinegar

¼ cup mayonnaise

½ cup sugar

1 teaspoon salt

½ teaspoon onion salt

½ teaspoon garlic salt

¼ teaspoon pepper

CHILLED CUCUMBER SALAD

Serves 8 to 10

This is a wonderful way to enjoy fresh garden cucumbers and satisfy your sweet tooth all at once. It keeps in the refrigerator for up to two weeks. Enjoy this cold, crispy salad on a hot summer day. I love the crunch of the sweet cucumbers.

10 cups peeled, thinly sliced fresh garden cucumbers

Ice water

2¼ cups sugar

¾ cup white vinegar

1 tablespoon salt

2 cups very thinly sliced onion

1. In a large stainless-steel bowl, cover the thinly sliced cucumbers with ice water. This is important, as it crisps the cucumbers. Cover and refrigerate for 2 hours.

2. While the cucumbers are chilling, whisk the sugar, vinegar, and salt together in a small pot over medium heat. Bring it to a low simmer, then remove from heat and allow to cool.

3. After 2 hours, remove the cucumbers from the refrigerator and drain off *all* the ice water. Add the thinly sliced onion to the cucumbers.

4. Carefully pour the sugar and vinegar mixture over the cucumbers and onions. Stir it all together well. Place this bowl back in the refrigerator for at least 1 hour to chill and completely absorb the sugar. Serve this salad cold at the table with a slotted spoon.

Note: To stretch this salad, I sometimes continue to add fresh crisped cucumber slices to the refrigerated dressing over the next week. It's one of my favorites!

GARDEN PASTA SALAD

AUTHENTIC RECIPE
THE HOMESTEAD
FROM THE HOMESTEAD

Serves 6 to 8

I have tried many pasta salads, and this one is still my tried-and-true favorite. It is so versatile; you can experiment with different pasta shapes and colors and a variety of chopped veggies to your liking.

1. Cook the pasta to al dente according to the package instructions. (To avoid soggy pasta, I undercook it by about 1 minute.) Rinse cooked pasta in cold water, drain well, and set aside.

2. Combine the Italian dressing, mayonnaise, and Parmesan cheese. Whisk it together well and pour over the cooked, drained pasta. Stir in the freshly chopped vegetables of your choice. Refrigerate the pasta salad for at least 4 hours before serving.

3. I like to garnish the top of this pasta salad with bell pepper rings and sprigs of fresh parsley.

3 cups uncooked rotini pasta

½ cup Italian dressing (I prefer Kraft Zesty Italian Dressing)

¼ cup mayonnaise

2 tablespoons grated Parmesan cheese

1½ cups finely chopped vegetables of your choice (I prefer a combination of red onion, cucumber, and red, yellow, and orange bell peppers)

Bell peppers, cut into rings, for garnish

Fresh parsley, for garnish

CHINESE CABBAGE SLAW

Serves 8 to 10

This salad is one of my favorites. It has lots of flavor and crunch! If you don't have napa cabbage, you can substitute a head of green cabbage in a pinch. Napa cabbage is also known as a Chinese cabbage and is generally more delicate in flavor and texture than green cabbage. To serve this slaw as a main dish, pair it with some air-fried popcorn chicken scattered on the top—it's delicious!

For the dressing

¾ cup canola oil

½ cup sugar

½ cup apple cider vinegar

2 tablespoons soy sauce

For the salad

¼ cup (½ stick) butter

2 (3-ounce) packages ramen noodles, crushed (discard the seasoning packets)

½ cup sliced almonds

½ cup sunflower seeds

1 head napa cabbage, finely chopped

1 bunch green onions, chopped

1. Combine the oil, sugar, vinegar, and soy sauce in a small saucepan. Bring to a boil and boil for 1 minute. Remove from heat and refrigerate.

2. Cook the butter, crushed ramen noodles, almonds, and sunflower seeds together until medium golden, stirring often so it doesn't burn. Remove from heat and allow to cool.

3. Just before serving, toss together the cabbage, onions, refrigerated dressing, and cooled crispy noodle mixture. Yum!

Note: The dressing can be made ahead and lasts in the refrigerator for a couple of weeks. The sautéed noodle mixture can also be made ahead. If I plan far enough ahead, I like to keep it ready in the freezer to pull out and add to the salad. It makes the slaw come together quickly and easily.

SNICKERS APPLE SALAD

Serves 10 to 12

This salad could almost pass as a dessert! It's delicious, especially in the fall. I look forward to picking fresh, crisp apples off the tree every year, and this recipe is always on the list of apple dishes to make. It is best served on the day it is made, but leftovers get eaten anytime around our home.

1. Whisk cold milk and instant pudding mix in a large bowl. Refrigerate for 15 minutes to thicken. When thickened, remove from the refrigerator and stir in whipped topping.

2. Using a rubber spatula, gently stir the candy bar pieces and apple pieces into the whipped pudding mixture. Scrape the edges and fill a serving bowl. I like to garnish the top with extra bite-size pieces of Snickers bar. Refrigerate until serving.

2 cups cold milk

½ cup instant French vanilla pudding mix

8 ounces frozen nondairy whipped topping

6 large Snickers candy bars, cut into bite-size pieces, plus more for topping

6 large apples (I prefer home-grown Honeycrisp), cut into bite-size pieces

STRAWBERRY LETTUCE SALAD

Serves 20

I still can't believe this is one of my favorite salads, because I typically do not think fruit and lettuce go together . . . especially with red onion. Our daughter Leandra requested this to be served at her wedding reception. It is such a delightful salad any time of year, but especially during the summer when fresh berries are abundant. The sugared almonds in this recipe are handy to keep in the freezer.

Dressing

½ cup mayonnaise

½ cup canola oil

¼ cup milk

¼ cup red wine vinegar

¼ cup strawberry jam

¼ cup sugar

3 tablespoons diced red or white onion

½ teaspoon salt

1 tablespoon poppy seeds

Sugared almonds

¼ cup (½ stick) butter

2 egg whites

½ cup sugar

2 cups slivered or sliced almonds

For the salad

2 pounds romaine lettuce, chopped

2 cups sliced fresh strawberries plus more for garnish

1 cup thinly sliced red onion (cut slices in half)

2 cups sugared almonds plus more for garnish

1 cup feta or mozzarella cheese (optional)

Dressing (amount to suit your taste)

1. *To make dressing:* Blend all the dressing ingredients *except* the poppy seeds together in the blender for 5 minutes. Gently stir in the poppy seeds, then refrigerate.

2. *To make sugared almonds:* Preheat the oven to 325°F. Place the butter on a large baking sheet and melt it in the warming oven. Beat the egg whites and sugar on high speed until the mixture stands in stiff peaks. Fold in the almonds. Spread this mixture in a thin layer over the melted butter. Bake at 325°F for 20 to 25 minutes, scraping and stirring every 5 minutes with a flat-bottomed metal spatula. The mixture will look strange and puffy, but that is normal. When the almond mixture is golden brown, remove it from the oven and let it cool completely. When cool, scrape it off the pan. I like to make these ahead and freeze them for an easy salad another day!

3. *To assemble salad:* Toss all the salad ingredients together. I like to garnish the top with extra berries and sugared almonds.

for he
satisfieth
the longing
soul, and
filleth the
hungry
soul with
goodness.

PSALM 107:9

SIDE DISHES

I had a difficult time scaling down my favorite side dishes! As I sorted through stacks of recipes, I realized that I had so many potato recipes. We love a good meat and potato meal, and my collection of potato dishes was too many to include all of them in this book. But I hope you enjoy the favorites that I've chosen.

CHUNKY APPLESAUCE

Serves 6 to 8

This chunky fall applesauce takes more effort than a smooth summer sauce, but it's worth it. I make larger batches and freeze the sauce in containers to enjoy all fall and winter. Fresh sauce is delicious, but we prefer this served when it is still partially frozen and a little slushy. It's a great side served along smoked sausage and potatoes on a crisp fall evening.

6 tree-ripened fall apples (I prefer Jonathan)

⅓ cup sugar

1 teaspoon ground cinnamon

1. Wash, peel, core, and quarter the apples. Place them in a large pot. *Partially* cover the apples with water. (For 6 apples, I would start with 3 cups water.) Cover and cook over medium heat until the apples are tender, stirring often so they don't scorch. If the mixture seems too thick and wants to stick, you can add additional water, 1 cup at a time. This amount will vary depending on the apples used. The goal is to not add too much water, or the sauce will be watery.

2. When the apples are tender and mushy, remove from heat and gently smash them using a potato masher. Leave some chunks of all sizes—this is what makes the sauce so good!

3. Stir in sugar and cinnamon while the mashed apples are still hot so the sugar dissolves. Let cool, package in small freezer containers of your choice, and freeze (or eat fresh!).

4. To serve frozen applesauce, remove the container from the freezer and let it stand at room temperature for about 1 hour. Remove the lid and chop the sauce up a little before putting it on the table. You may also sprinkle on a little more cinnamon, if preferred.

AUTUMN BAKED APPLES

Serves 8 to 10

Any kind of baking apple works for this recipe, but I especially love tree-ripened Jonathan apples. If there is extra sauce left over after the apples have been eaten, this can be used over pancakes as a delicious twist on pancake syrup.

1. Preheat the oven to 350°F. Wash, core, and quarter the apples and place them skin side up in a greased 13 x 9-inch baking dish or a 12-inch cast iron skillet.

2. In a separate microwavable bowl, combine the brown sugar, corn syrup, cornstarch, cold water, and cinnamon. Whisk together well. Heat in the microwave for 3 to 5 minutes, stopping every minute to whisk the mixture until it starts to thicken. Pour this sauce over the apples in the pan. Bake, uncovered, at 350°F for 45 to 60 minutes until the apples are tender and able to be easily poked with a sharp knife. Remove from the oven and let the apples cool to lukewarm to serve.

6 large baking apples

½ cup packed brown sugar

½ cup light corn syrup

3 tablespoons cornstarch or Thermflo

1½ cups cold water

1 tablespoon ground cinnamon

SLICED FROZEN PEACHES

1 bushel fresh peaches yields 14 to 15 quarts

When the girls were young and I was a busy stay-at-home mom, I did a lot of canning and freezing. As time changes rivers, so goes the course of our lives. Now that it is just Mike and me around the table, I no longer can and freeze like I once did. However, freezing fresh, juicy peaches is something that I will always continue to do. We could eat these peaches every single meal, but we reserve them for Sunday morning breakfast when weekend guests visit. They are that special!

For the best flavor, use fresh, juicy peaches when they are in season. To avoid frustration, use "free stone" peaches, meaning their pit removes easily. Not all peaches are created equal! Here in Indiana, we have access to Michigan Red Haven peaches, and you just can't beat them.

I purchase fresh peaches each season, either through our local IGA grocery store or at a farm stand, then wait for them to ripen. To do this, spread newspaper on the counter and carefully lay out the peaches in a single layer. Be careful not to drop or bruise them. For optimal ripening, it is best to leave them in an air-conditioned space. Watch the ripening progress of the peaches closely. Within a few days, they are usually soft to the touch and ideal for freezing.

1 bushel fresh, ripe peaches

4 pounds sugar

2 to 3 tablespoons Fruit-Fresh Produce Protector*

1. Wash, halve, pit, and peel the peaches with a sharp paring knife. Be careful not to gouge the peach too deep, or you will waste a lot of the good part! Slice peeled peaches into a large 10-quart bowl. Add 4 cups sugar and 1 tablespoon Fruit-Fresh Produce Protector to each large bowl. Stir well with a large spoon. Let the peaches stand for 5 to 10 minutes, then stir again. Natural juices will begin to ooze out of the peaches, creating a delicious light juice. (If you want to enjoy truly fresh, delicious peaches, now is the time to load up a serving bowl and indulge. They never get better! Mike loves them over a mound of vanilla ice cream, but I prefer to enjoy their flavor as they are.)

2. If there are any left (wink, wink), fill pint- or quart-size freezer containers and snap on the lids. Label the containers with the current date, then stack them in the freezer. They will keep for 1 year or longer.

3. To serve, remove a container of frozen peaches from the freezer about 2 hours before mealtime. Pour the partially thawed peaches into a serving bowl, allowing the juices to flow over the slushy mound of pure deliciousness! We love them served partially slushy. Just before serving, I sometimes add fresh blueberries or strawberries or any other fresh fruit for a delicious and colorful combination.

* Fruit-Fresh Produce Protector from Ball is a food preservative that protects the color and flavor of fruit.

BAKED POTATOES WITH LOADED TOPPING

Serves 6

Baked potatoes pair well with any type of grilled meat. They can be served the simple way with butter, salt, and pepper—or for extra special flavor and presentation, I like to serve them with this baked potato topping. It can turn any basic meal into something fancy!

1. Preheat the oven to 350°F. Poke each clean potato thoroughly with a sharp knife to keep the potatoes from exploding in the oven.

2. Using clean hands, rub the potatoes thoroughly with vegetable shortening. Yes, they will be greasy! (I have also used butter-flavored vegetable shortening, and it is delicious as well.)

3. Place each shortening-coated whole potato into a lightly greased disposable aluminum foil pan (for easy cleanup).* Sprinkle each potato with coarse salt. Bake at 350°F for about 1½ hours or less. After 1 hour, check the potatoes. If they can easily be squeezed, they are thoroughly baked and can be removed from the oven. Serve with butter, salt, and pepper or with the baked potato topping.

4. *To make topping:* Mix the ingredients together in a small bowl. Serve alongside fresh baked potatoes for an all-in-one loaded potato topping. Garnish with finely shredded cheddar cheese.

6 large russet potatoes, washed and dried

Vegetable shortening

Coarse salt

Loaded topping

1¼ cups sour cream

5 tablespoons butter, at room temperature

¾ cup fried bacon pieces

⅓ cup chopped green onion (I like to use part of the greens)

Finely shredded cheddar cheese, for garnish

---

* If I do not have a foil pan, a simple sheet of aluminum foil on the oven rack does the trick.

BROWN BUTTER RED POTATOES

Serves 4 to 6

I first experienced browned butter drizzled over a mound of fluffy mashed potatoes while enjoying a delightful dinner around our Amish friends' table. Mike and I met Ivan and Esther Miller in Ohio years ago when Ivan was the cabinet salesman we worked with when we built our home! As Ivan casually asked about our family, we told him that we had five girls—including one set of twins. He broke into a grin and said, "My wife and I have five girls—including a set of twins!" All ten girls were of similar ages! Our families made connections, and through the years, we frequently enjoy visiting them and their amazing variety store, Summit Valley Fabrics in Apple Creek, Ohio. It is convenient that our daughter Leandra and her husband Kevin live on a dairy farm nearby—so we get out there on occasion!

6 red potatoes, with skins on

½ cup (1 stick) butter

Salt and pepper

1. Wash the potatoes and place them in a large pot on the stove. Completely cover them with water. Cover the pot and bring to a boil. Reduce the heat to a gentle bubble, slightly cock the lid, and continue to boil gently until the potatoes are tender.

2. *To make brown butter:* While potatoes are boiling, place butter in a small, shallow pot on the stove. Melt the butter and let it gently sizzle over medium heat, stirring often with a rubber spatula. When you see the butter begin to puff up and form white foam, it is ready to be removed from the heat. This will take several minutes. If you quickly scrape back the foam, you will see clear browned butter underneath. It may contain little flecks of toasted milk solids. I like to use all of this (including the browned sediment) over my potatoes. That's where the flavor is!

3. When the potatoes are tender and the butter is browned, drain the hot potatoes. Cut each potato in half or fourths and drizzle the brown butter over the potatoes. Gently toss with a rubber spatula. Season with salt and pepper. Serve immediately while hot.

BUTTERY MASHED POTATOES

Serves 8 to 10

These creamy real mashed potatoes can be made ahead and refrigerated if needed. Always remember to keep your peeled potato chunks covered in water while you peel the remaining potatoes. This will prevent them from turning dark.

1. Place peeled and cubed potatoes in a pot and cover with water. Bring to a boil. Reduce heat and cook, uncovered, for 15 to 20 minutes, or until potatoes are very tender. When the potatoes are tender, drain and return them to the pot, but turn off the heat. Using an electric hand mixer, whip the tender potatoes while hot. (*Tip:* For a fluffy texture, always whip potatoes as soon as you drain them. If you let them cool slightly before whipping, they will get gummy.)

2. Whip the cream cheese, sour cream, butter, onion powder, garlic powder, salt, and pepper into the potatoes. If the potatoes seem a little stiff, add a tiny drizzle of milk. Serve piping hot with prepared brown butter drizzled over the top of the bowl of potatoes.

3 pounds Yukon Gold or russet potatoes, peeled and cubed (you may also use red potatoes, but do not peel them)

1 (8-ounce) package cream cheese, at room temperature

½ cup sour cream

½ cup (1 stick) butter, cut into slices

1½ teaspoons onion powder

1 teaspoon garlic powder

1 teaspoon salt

½ teaspoon pepper

Milk (optional)

¼ cup brown butter*

* To make brown butter: Place ¼ cup butter in a small, shallow pot on the stove. Melt the butter and let it gently sizzle over medium heat, stirring often with a rubber spatula. When the butter puffs up and foams, it is ready to be removed from the heat. (This will take several minutes.) If you quickly scrape back the foam, you will see clear browned butter underneath along with flecks of toasted milk solids.

LOADED MASHED POTATO CASSEROLE

1 cup shredded cheddar cheese

3 green onions, chopped

1 cup fried bacon pieces

Preheat the oven to 350°F. To serve these mashed potatoes as a loaded mashed potato casserole, place hot whipped potatoes (without or without brown butter) in a greased 13 x 9-inch pan. Sprinkle the top with shredded cheddar cheese, chopped green onions, and bacon pieces. Heat, uncovered, at 350°F until the potatoes are heated through and the cheese is melted.

FRIED POTATOES

Serves 6 to 8

This is my go-to potato recipe when I'm in a hurry. It can be on the table in about half an hour and is a wonderful complement to grilled burgers or steak on a hot summer night. Mike prefers these served with ketchup, but I like them with ranch dressing.

½ cup (1 stick) butter

6 large potatoes, washed, dried, quartered, then cut into ½-inch pieces (I peel the potatoes only if the skin is thick or blemished)

Garlic salt, as desired

Pepper, as desired

Toppings such as shredded cheddar cheese, green onions, fried bacon pieces, ranch dressing (optional)

1. In a shallow skillet, melt the butter over low heat. Add the potatoes. Stir well to coat with butter, then season to your liking with garlic salt and pepper. Cover the skillet and let it steam over medium heat for about 20 minutes, stirring frequently to prevent the potatoes from sticking to the bottom of the skillet.

2. When the potatoes are tender, remove the lid and continue to heat on medium to crisp the potatoes. You may need to decrease the temperature to low and let them slowly get a little crispy. I usually move the whole sizzling skillet right onto the table to serve.

3. For a different twist, sprinkle shredded cheddar cheese, green onions, and fried bacon pieces over the top of the hot potatoes. Drizzle with ranch dressing at the table. These are so good!

PARMESAN BAKED POTATOES

Serves 6 to 8

If you're looking for a side dish that is both easy to prepare and tastes delicious, this one is ideal.

1. Preheat the oven to 400°F. Pour the melted butter into a 13 x 9-inch baking pan. In a separate bowl, stir together the Parmesan cheese, garlic salt, and pepper. Sprinkle this mixture evenly over the melted butter. Arrange the potatoes, cut side down, on top.

2. Bake, uncovered, at 400°F for 45 minutes, or until potatoes are tender and the cut side is a little crispy and golden.

3. These are delicious served plain or with Loaded Topping for Baked Potatoes (p. 117).

6 tablespoons (¾ stick) butter, melted

3 tablespoons grated Parmesan cheese

¼ teaspoon garlic salt

⅛ teaspoon pepper

8 medium unpeeled red potatoes, halved lengthwise

GRANDMA ISCH'S HOMEMADE NOODLES

Serves 6 to 8

These hearty, wholesome noodles are worth the work and drying time! You'll need a pasta maker machine and some space to dry the noodles for several days. I use a YASHE Manual Pasta Maker Machine. There are other similar brands on the market.

To make noodles

1 dozen whole eggs plus 2 egg yolks

Yellow food color (optional)

6 to 8 cups all-purpose flour

To cook noodles

6 tablespoons (¾ stick) butter, divided

½ teaspoon salt plus more for serving

About 8 cups frozen dried noodles

Braislee Breadcrumbs

½ cup (1 stick) butter

4 cups fine blended breadcrumbs (my mom used bread heels if she had them)

MAKING NOODLES

1. Crack the 1 dozen whole eggs into a large bowl and add the 2 egg yolks. Whisk together well. To give the noodles a little brighter shade of yellow, add a few drops of yellow food color, if desired. Add flour to create a somewhat stiff, sticky dough. I never measure . . . just keep adding flour until the dough is workable with clean hands and thick enough to cut the dough into four equal pieces.

2. Shape each of the four pieces of egg noodle dough into a log about 2 inches in diameter. You may need to knead in a little more flour as you do this. Cut a 1-inch slice of dough from a log. Line a 9-inch pie pan with approximately ¼ to ½ cup flour, then place the 1-inch dough puck inside, pressing and flattening as you work in the flour.

3. Run this piece through a pasta maker machine using the sheet roller function, starting at the largest number and continuing to decrease the number until you are eventually left with a very thin #2-setting sheet of noodle dough. (As you make a thinner and thinner sheet, dredge it with additional flour as needed.)

4. Move this thin sheet of dough onto large, clean towels to begin drying in preparation to cut the fine noodles. Repeat this process again and again with the remaining dough pucks until all the dough has been sheeted and is drying. By this time, the first sheets will be ready to cut.

5. Move the hand crank over to the noodle width setting of choice. (We always use the skinniest option.) Begin feeding each sheet of dough through the cutter and watch the long, thin strands of noodle dough begin to pile up.

6. Carefully move the fine strands over to a table laid with a clean sheet or towels. Now the final drying process begins. You can expect the noodles to be fully dry within 48 hours.

STORING NOODLES

When the noodles are fully dry (this will likely take 48 hours), they can be cooked and enjoyed or gently packaged in 2- to 4-quart freezer-safe containers and frozen for other meals or special occasions.

COOKING NOODLES

1. In a large stockpot, bring 6 to 8 cups water to a rapid boil. Add 4 tablespoons (½ stick) of the butter and ½ teaspoon salt. Remove about 8 cups loosely packed noodles from the freezer. Carefully add the thin noodles, stirring with a long-handled spoon. Cover, then reduce the heat to medium-low. Simmer and cook for about 10 minutes, watching the water content in the pot. If it begins to boil dry before 10 minutes, add another 1 cup water so the cooking process can continue.

2. Once the noodles are tender, drain any excess water and toss with the remaining 2 tablespoons butter and salt as desired. Fill your serving bowl and top with toasted Braislee Breadcrumbs to enjoy!

3. *To make Braislee Breadcrumbs:* In a large skillet, melt the butter and mix in the breadcrumbs. Gently let them toast over medium-low heat. When they are toasted and golden, remove from heat and store in a freezer container. These can be thawed 1 to 2 hours in advance of serving the noodles.

NOODLE DAY

The tradition of homemade noodles runs deep in our family. There was never a holiday meal at Grandpa and Grandma Isch's without Grandma's homemade noodles. Hers weren't the thick hand-cut noodles you may think of when it comes to this classic treat; hers were very thin and delicate and oh so yummy. Grandma made "braislee" to put on top of the steaming mound of noodles. I'm not sure where that word originates, but that's what we always called the fine, toasted breadcrumbs that were used as a buttery, crunchy topping.

My mom carried on this tradition, and I remember the excitement we felt when Mom dug out the hand-crank noodle maker from deep within the closet, signaling the arrival of Noodle Day. She started by cracking all the eggs and then mixing in flour until she had a thick yellow dough. Soon, the long, narrow, paper-thin sheets of noodle dough were cranked out and placed on clean towels either spread out on the table or hanging over a chair.

When the dough had dried just the right amount, it was time to watch the magic happen! As the long thin sheets of dough were cranked through the noodle maker, the strands of cut noodles piled into a heap on the front side of the cutter. Mom gently lifted the noodles over to the table to dry. It was important to spread them out for proper drying. As they dried, we fluffed them by gently lifting to spread them out, but we had to be so careful not to crush or break any of the precious noodles.

After giving them a couple of days to completely dry, it was time to loosely pack them away in old Schwan's ice cream buckets to be frozen and used for special occasions like holiday meals. Mom was always asked to bring her noodles to the Hartter Thanksgiving and Christmas dinners. Occasionally, we were treated to homemade noodles on the table at home for no special reason, other than to enjoy this delectable treat—what a special day that always was!

Today, I love to crank out my own homemade noodles, and I look forward to carrying on this tradition with my girls and grandchildren. I hope that they, too, will always treasure the nostalgia of this dish.

and Jesus
said unto them,
I am the bread
of life: he that
cometh to me shall
never hunger;
and he that
believeth on me
shall never thirst.

JOHN 6:35

CHEESY CARROTS

Serves 8 to 10

These cheesy carrots win my heart every time. The cheese sauce is so easy and flavorful, and the buttered cornflakes on the top add so much flavorful crunch. If you don't have cornflakes, you can substitute buttered crushed cracker crumbs sprinkled over the top for the last 10 minutes of baking time.

4 pounds petite baby carrots

¼ cup (½ stick) butter, melted

4 cups crushed cornflakes cereal

1 teaspoon packed brown sugar

1 (15-ounce) jar process cheese sauce (I use Cheese Whiz)

½ cup (1 stick) additional butter

¼ teaspoon garlic powder

⅛ teaspoon pepper

1. Preheat the oven to 350°F. Cook baby carrots in boiling water just until tender. Drain well and set aside.

2. In a separate bowl, combine the ¼ cup melted butter, crushed cornflakes, and brown sugar. Stir together until well mixed. Set aside.

3. Melt the cheese sauce, ½ cup additional butter, garlic powder, and pepper together in a small microwavable bowl until smooth. Pour over the drained carrots and toss gently with a rubber spatula.

4. Spread the cheesy carrots into a greased 13 x 9-inch baking pan. Top with buttered crushed cornflakes and heat at 350°F for 30 minutes.

CREAMED ASPARAGUS

Serves 6 to 8

Two garden foods that I could hardly choke down as a very young child are now two of my favorites—asparagus and rhubarb. When I was growing up, Mom made creamed asparagus and served it over toast. My appreciation for this dish was a later gift in life, as I began to experiment with the fresh garden crop of asparagus that poked through the soil the first spring after Mike and I moved onto the Bahler homeplace. I enjoyed experimenting with it, and this dish became a favorite in our home. Unlike me as a child, the girls loved it when I served creamed asparagus and toast.

1. Place chopped fresh asparagus in a small pan on the stove. Cover with water. Bring to a low boil and cook until tender—do not overcook, or the asparagus will be mushy. Remove from heat and drain the water very well. Set aside.

2. Mix melted butter, milk, flour, garlic powder, salt, and pepper in a microwave-safe bowl, then heat the mixture in the microwave, whisking periodically, until it thickens into a smooth white sauce. When it thickens, add cubes of process cheese spread and stir until melted.

3. Combine asparagus, hard-cooked eggs, and hot cheese sauce. Stir gently with a rubber spatula until well combined. Serve this cheesy, creamed asparagus over hot toast at the table.

1 pound fresh asparagus, washed and chopped into 1-inch pieces (stop cutting at the tough part of the stem)

6 tablespoons (¾ stick) butter, melted

2½ cups milk

6 tablespoons flour

¼ teaspoon garlic powder

¼ teaspoon salt

⅛ teaspoon pepper

½ pound process cheese spread, cubed

8 hard-cooked eggs, chopped

Slices of hot toast, to serve

GREEN BEANS AND CARAMELIZED BACON

Serves 6 to 8

Fresh garden green beans are best when they are in season. Otherwise, I use either frozen green beans or canned green beans with this recipe. We like lots of fried bacon on top of our green beans, so I don't skimp—sometimes I hear guests comment that they like the bacon that is served with the green beans. I usually fry up a pound of bacon at a time. If I don't use it all, the remainder can be frozen and used for another meal. Use the amount you prefer.

1 pound fresh or frozen green beans, or 2 (14.5-ounce) cans, drained

¼ cup (½ stick) butter, cubed

Lawry's or another seasoned salt, to taste

Caramelized bacon

1 pound raw bacon, cut into small pieces

½ cup diced onion

2 tablespoons (¼ stick) butter

1 tablespoon packed brown sugar

1. *If using fresh or frozen green beans:* Cook beans in boiling water just until crisp-tender. Drain completely. Toss hot beans with cubed butter. Add seasoned salt and toss until the butter is melted.

If using canned green beans: Drain beans and heat gently on the stove. Toss with butter and seasoned salt until butter is melted.

2. *To make caramelized bacon:* Fry the bacon pieces together with the onion, butter, and brown sugar in a small skillet on the stove, stirring often, until the bacon is crispy. Drain any excess drippings.

3. Serve caramelized bacon over the top of the hot buttered green beans.

ROASTED VEGGIES

Serves 16 to 18

For those who struggle to get their veggies in, this may be one way to enjoy them. You will need five pounds of chopped fresh vegetables—I vary the vegetables according to what I have on hand. Be creative, and think color! These are delicious and so colorful on the table.

1. Preheat the oven to 450°F.

2. Place the chopped vegetables in a large bowl.

3. In a separate small bowl, whisk together the remaining ingredients. Pour this mixture over the chopped vegetables and stir well until the vegetables are evenly coated.

4. Spread the seasoned vegetables out onto a lightly greased 15 x 10-inch baking sheet. Roast, uncovered, at 450°F for 20 to 30 minutes, or until vegetables are crisp-tender and starting to become a little charred on the tips. Using a flat metal spatula, stir the vegetables once or twice during the roasting time.

5. If desired, sprinkle a little salt and freshly grated Parmesan on top of the vegetables just before serving.

5 pounds various fresh vegetables, cleaned and chopped (use a blend—for example, broccoli, cauliflower, red onion, mushrooms, baby carrots, bell peppers, asparagus, snow peas)

¼ cup grated Parmesan cheese plus additional for sprinkling

¼ cup olive oil

2 tablespoons balsamic vinegar

1 tablespoon Better Than Bouillon Seasoned Vegetable Base, or ½ teaspoon granulated chicken bouillon

¾ teaspoon minced fresh garlic

½ teaspoon Italian seasoning

⅛ teaspoon pepper

MOM'S POTLUCK BAKED BEANS

Serves 20 to 24

I grew up in a small community with a small church congregation, so we loved it when guests visited—that usually meant there would be a church potluck! I have fond memories of attending these large communal meals growing up. This recipe was passed on to my mom by Eileen Bahr. We knew Eileen would always bring her large pot of baked beans, and they were delicious. Mom has carried on the tradition of taking these baked beans to church potlucks. I love to serve baked beans in the summertime with a good burger meal.

1 (114-ounce) #10 can pork and beans, *mostly* drained

1 pound bacon, fried and diced

½ cup chopped onion

2½ cups packed dark brown sugar

1¾ cups ketchup

2 tablespoons molasses

1 tablespoon white vinegar

1 tablespoon dry mustard

2 teaspoons liquid smoke

1. Preheat the oven to 300°F. Stir all the ingredients together well. Place in a large roasting pan or a large, oven-safe roasting pan. Bake, uncovered, at 300°F for 2½ hours. Stir a few times during baking. Skim off any bacon fat that floats to the top.

Note: I have found that these beans seem to thicken and become more flavorful if prepared a day ahead and reheated on the day of the potluck or other meal. This makes a large batch, but they can be made and frozen in small quantities. Pull out, thaw, and heat to serve as needed.

BREADS, MUFFINS, COFFEE CAKES, AND ROLLS

I think I could live on bread alone! Don't let fear of yeast breads and rolls scare you from trying these recipes. Sometimes it takes a little practice, and yes, I still have flops. The experience of enjoying freshly baked bread hot out of the oven by slathering it with real soft butter—watching it melt into the piping hot bread—and popping it into your mouth is something that can't be explained. Never ruin fresh bread by substituting margarine in any form. Butter truly does make everything better!

YEAST BREADS AND ROLLS

Many people are skeptical about trying yeast breads and rolls. It can seem like a long, complicated process to beginners. With some practice, you will become more comfortable with the techniques that yield delicious results—and fill your home with the most delicious scents. I find that working with yeast dough is both therapeutic and satisfying.

I've jotted down some tips that have helped me through the years. I've had plenty of flop batches, but one thing is for certain . . . there is always another chance. There's also a chance that others might think your flops are delicious! So roll up your sleeves, and let's get started.

- I use *instant yeast* in all my bread recipes. SAF Instant is my go-to brand; it comes in a 1-pound vacuum-sealed package. Other brands of instant yeast in small packets are available in grocery stores. One packet of dry instant yeast equals 2¼ teaspoons. Instant yeast allows you to shape your bread for one rise, rather than two, and it saves precious time. There is no need to dissolve instant yeast in warm water. Toss it in with your dry ingredients and add the water with the other liquid ingredients.
- Never use hot water when making bread. It will kill the yeast, and the bread will not rise. Lukewarm water, about 105°F to 110°F, is ideal.
- Find a warm place in your house or kitchen for your bread to rise. This might be near the woodstove if you have one. Just make sure it isn't too hot.
- Brush hot yeast breads with melted butter after baking. This adds extra flavor and gives the bread extra shine.
- I use the flour measurements in recipes as a guide, but you must ultimately go by the feel of yeast dough. You want it to feel a little tacky—it will be ready when your fingers kind of stick to it but don't become completely gunky.
- Bread flour isn't necessary to make yeast breads and rolls. Any all-purpose flour will work fine.
- Most of my yeast bread recipes instruct bakers to drizzle a little canola oil into the dough just before shutting off the mixer. This helps the mass of dough release from the bowl a little better. In our Homestead production kitchen with its large mixing bowls, this is extremely helpful. A "little" oil can depend on the size of your dough mass, but for home recipes, it is generally just a trickle—no more than 2 tablespoons to ¼ cup.
- To see if sweet rolls are done baking, use a small paring knife and gently lift the center portion of one of the rolls. I usually try to pick one near the center of the pan. Lift gently. If it has a stretchy, doughy appearance, the rolls need to be baked longer. If the test roll looks like fluffy bread, the rolls are done.
- Never store bread in the refrigerator. The starch molecules recrystallize quickly at refrigerator temperatures and cause the bread to go stale much faster when refrigerated. Bread is best eaten at room temperature within a couple of days, or store it in the freezer to ensure freshness.

"And Jesus said unto them, I am the bread of life: he that cometh to me shall never hunger;
and he that believeth on me shall never thirst." —John 6:35

BUTTERED FARMHOUSE CORN BREAD

Serves 16 to 20

A hefty piece of this corn bread, still warm from the oven, is a perfect complement to a steamy bowl of chili or a meal of smoked sausage and potatoes. To bump it up to the next level, spread warm portions with soft butter and drizzle with honey or maple syrup. If I serve this corn bread with smoked sausage, I prefer it with maple syrup—it melts in your mouth!

Now that it is just Mike and me at home, we don't need so much in one setting. You can portion the corn bread into freezer containers and freeze them for another meal or two. Reheat in the microwave to serve.

1 cup (2 sticks) butter, at room temperature

1½ cups sugar

5 eggs

2½ cups milk

3½ cups flour

1½ cups yellow or white cornmeal

2 tablespoons plus 1 teaspoon baking powder

1½ teaspoons salt

1. Preheat the oven to 325°F. In a large bowl, beat together the soft butter and sugar. In a separate bowl, whisk together the eggs and milk. In another bowl, combine the flour, cornmeal, baking powder, and salt; add this mixture to the butter mixture, alternating with the egg mixture.

2. Spread the batter evenly into a greased 18 x 13-inch half-sheet pan. Bake at 325°F for 30 to 35 minutes, or until a wooden pick inserted in the center comes out clean. Portions of corn bread are delicious served hot from the oven.

GLAZED CINNAMON COFFEE CAKE

Serves 10 to 12

Our family's favorite coffee cake!

1. Preheat the oven to 325°F. Beat the butter and sugar on high with a hand beater; then add eggs and vanilla, beating well. Continue to add the flour, baking soda, baking powder, salt, and buttermilk, beating as you go.

2. Spread half the batter evenly into a greased 13 x 9-inch baking pan. In a small bowl, mix together the cinnamon filling ingredients and sprinkle half the mixture evenly over the batter in the pan. Spread the rest of the batter on top, being careful to spread evenly and completely to the edges. Sprinkle the top evenly with the remaining cinnamon filling.

3. Bake at 325°F for 35 to 45 minutes, or until the center is set and a wooden pick inserted in the center comes out clean.

4. While the coffee cake is baking, make the icing by mixing all the ingredients together. Drizzle icing over the coffee cake while it is still warm.

1 cup (2 sticks) butter, at room temperature (*not* melted)

1 cup sugar

2 eggs

1 teaspoon vanilla extract

2 cups flour

1 teaspoon baking soda

1 teaspoon baking powder

1 teaspoon salt

1 cup buttermilk*

Cinnamon filling

¼ cup packed brown sugar

3 tablespoons granulated sugar

1 teaspoon ground cinnamon

Icing

1 cup powdered sugar

2 tablespoons butter, melted

1½ teaspoons milk

½ teaspoon vanilla extract

* If you do not have buttermilk, you can make a buttermilk substitute with milk and vinegar: Pour 1 tablespoon white vinegar into a small liquid measuring cup. Add milk to the 1-cup line. Stir gently, then let this mixture sit for 5 minutes as the milk "sours" and thickens.

GRANDMA HARTTER'S CINNAMON POPPY SEED BREAD

Yields 2 loaves

We love this quick and easy poppy seed bread. It is sweet and so delicious sliced into thin slices while cold. Tip: Always store poppy seeds in the refrigerator or freezer. They are high in oil and tend to go rancid if left at room temperature for extended periods.

1 cup sugar

2 teaspoons ground cinnamon

1 (15.25-ounce) box yellow cake mix

½ cup instant vanilla pudding mix

½ cup canola oil

½ cup pineapple orange juice

½ cup water

4 eggs

1 teaspoon almond extract

¼ cup poppy seeds

1. Preheat the oven to 325°F. Mix together the sugar and ground cinnamon. Grease two 6¼ x 3¾ x 2¾-inch loaf pans with cooking spray and sprinkle with the cinnamon-sugar mixture. Tap out the excess to use later.

2. In a mixing bowl, stir together the cake mix and pudding mix. Add canola oil, juice, and water. Add the eggs one at a time, beating well. Add the almond extract and poppy seeds.

3. Pour the batter evenly into the two prepared bread pans. Tap the pans lightly on the counter to remove air bubbles from the batter.

4. Bake at 325°F for 40 to 45 minutes, or until the center is fully baked and a wooden pick inserted in the center comes out clean. Remove the pans from the oven and let them cool for 5 to 10 minutes. Carefully remove the loaves from the pans while they are still warm, then roll them in additional cinnamon-sugar mixture, coating the bread on all sides.

5. This bread freezes well—I like to wrap the fully cooled loaves tightly with plastic wrap and freeze. They slice so nicely when they are still partially frozen.

MOM'S BUBBLE BREAD

Yields 1 (12-cup) Bundt pan ring

I am certain that this recipe was one of the very first I ever learned to make, as Mom served it often. It is a quick addition to the evening dinner. This recipe begins with refrigerated biscuit dough. I have also served it on the breakfast table as a sweet bread.

½ cup (1 stick) butter

1 cup sugar

2 teaspoons ground cinnamon

2 (16.3-ounce) tubes biscuits (I prefer Grands! Flaky Layers Original Biscuits)

1. Preheat the oven to 350°F. Thoroughly grease a 12-cup Bundt pan with cooking spray. Melt the butter in a small bowl and set aside. In a separate small bowl, combine the sugar and cinnamon and mix well.

2. Open the two cans of biscuits. Dip each biscuit into the melted butter, letting the excess drip off for a few seconds. Roll the buttered biscuit dough into the cinnamon-sugar mixture. Completely cover all sides of the biscuit.

3. Stand the biscuits up in a line in the Bundt pan. Two cans of biscuits will fill one Bundt pan.

4. Bake at 350°F for 35 to 40 minutes, or until the biscuits puff up and are not doughy. They should be baked to a moderately golden color. Remove from the oven and immediately invert the pan onto a serving plate. This bread is best enjoyed while warm as a pull-apart bread.

OUR FAVORITE BRAN MUFFINS

Yields 24 muffins

These bran muffins remind me of a muffin that our elementary school cooks served to us. It evokes sweet memories of Madison Elementary every time I make them. I also remember the hot buttered bread that they served in the lunch line. The bottom crust was always so crunchy and buttery—my favorite part!

1 cup wheat bran (I prefer Bob's Red Mill brand)

1 cup boiling water

2 eggs, beaten

½ cup (1 stick) butter, at room temperature

2 cups buttermilk*

2½ cups flour

1¼ cups sugar

2½ teaspoons baking soda

½ teaspoon salt

1. Preheat the oven to 400°F. Stir together the wheat bran and boiling water and let stand for 10 minutes. Combine this mixture and the remaining ingredients in a bowl, being careful not to overmix. (*Note:* This batter will be thin.) Fill 24 paper-lined muffin tins with ⅓ cup batter each.

2. Bake at 400°F for 13 to 14 minutes. The muffins should be light golden and spring back when fully baked.

3. These are delicious warm. Serve with additional soft butter and let it melt into the muffin.

* If you do not have buttermilk, you can make a buttermilk substitute with milk and vinegar: Pour 2 tablespoons white vinegar into a small liquid measuring cup. Add milk to the 2-cup line. Stir gently, then let this mixture sit for 5 minutes as the milk "sours" and thickens.

PUMPKIN CHOCOLATE CHIP MUFFINS

Yields 24 to 30 muffins

When the air turns crisp and leaves start to fall, we know it is time to bring out these delicious muffins! They freeze well to enjoy later. This is a treasured recipe that was given to me by Lynnette Bahler after our house fire.

1. Preheat the oven to 350°F.

2. Mix together the pumpkin puree, eggs, vegetable oil, flour, sugar, baking soda, baking powder, cinnamon, and salt. Gently fold in the milk chocolate chips. Fill paper-lined muffin tins about two-thirds full and bake at 350°F for 16 to 20 minutes, just until centers are set.

1 (16-ounce) can pumpkin puree

4 eggs

1½ cups vegetable oil

3 cups flour

2 cups sugar

2 teaspoons baking soda

2 teaspoons baking powder

1½ teaspoons ground cinnamon

1 teaspoon salt

2 cups milk chocolate chips

BUTTERHORN DINNER ROLLS

Yields 2 dozen rolls

Homemade dinner rolls were always on the Thanksgiving table at my grandma Isch's home along with her homemade noodles and a heaping mound of fluffy, scratch-made mashed potatoes. Our meals were, without doubt, heavy on carbs, but oh, how delicious—and so satisfying and comforting. This dough can be shaped any way you like—feel free to experiment with your own style.

½ cup (1 stick) butter, softened

4 eggs, divided

5 to 6 cups flour, divided

4 teaspoons instant yeast

9 tablespoons sugar

1 teaspoon salt

1¼ cups warm water

Canola oil

Additional butter, melted, for brushing

1. Preheat the oven to 350°F. In a stand mixer fitted with a dough hook, beat together the butter, 3 of the eggs, 2 cups of the flour, instant yeast, sugar, salt, and warm water. Turn the speed down to low and slowly add the remaining 3 to 4 cups of flour until the kneaded dough cleans the side of the mixer and is soft and pliable. Just before shutting off the mixer, drizzle in a little canola oil to coat the dough ball.

2. Cut dough into two even pieces (weighed on a kitchen scale, each half should measure about 1.7 pounds). Shape each piece into a nice ball. Using a rolling pin, roll one ball into an even 16-inch circle on a lightly greased countertop. In a small bowl, whisk the remaining egg. Brush the dough lightly with the beaten egg. Using a pizza cutter, cut the circle into 12 wedges. Starting from the outside edge, roll up each wedge into a tight butterhorn-style roll. As you roll up each wedge, you will end with the point. Seal the point into the roll by giving it a hard pinch. Place the point side down on a greased baking sheet. Repeat with the remaining ball of dough.

3. Bake at 350°F for 20 to 25 minutes, or until the rolls are lightly golden. Remove the rolls from the oven and immediately brush with melted butter.

VARIATION: BASIC ROUND DINNER ROLLS

To make basic round dinner rolls, cut dough into blobs that weigh about 2.25 ounces each, then shape them into smooth rolls. Grease three 8-inch round cake pans with cooking spray. Place 8 dough balls in each pan (place 7 on the outside and 1 in the middle). Bake as directed.

whether
therefore ye eat,
or drink, or
whatsoever ye
do, do all
to the glory
of God.

1 CORINTHIANS 10:31

HONEY BUTTER DINNER ROLLS

Yields 8 dinner rolls

We love dinner rolls, and we love butter. When the girls were young, I created the combination of dinner rolls and honey butter and ended up with these melt-in-your-mouth delights. The girls still talk about these buttery rolls, and now our sons-in-law enjoy them with us too. There are never any left on the table!

1. Preheat the oven to 350°F. Leave the baked rolls in the pan. Using a small, serrated knife, cut the rolls apart at all the seams, and cut around the edge of the pan.

2. Melt ¾ cup Honey Butter to liquid butter. Slowly drizzle the melted honey butter over the pan of rolls. Drizzle in the cracks around the edges, continuing until you have drizzled all the melted butter. It will pool on top of the rolls, and they will appear to be super saturated. This is normal!

3. Carefully cover the pan tightly with aluminum foil. Heat the covered pan at 350°F for 20 minutes. Remove from the oven, carefully remove the foil, and serve immediately. They are so pillowy soft and buttery—they might be less messy if eaten with a fork!

1 (8-inch) round pan baked Dinner Rolls (p. 158), prepared as basic round rolls

¾ cup Honey Butter (see sidebar)

HONEY BUTTER

Yields 2 cups

If you love a good, sweet honey butter on fresh homemade bread, this recipe never fails.

1 cup (2 sticks) butter, at room temperature

½ cup honey

1 tablespoon canola oil

2 tablespoons powdered sugar

½ teaspoon ground cinnamon

Using an electric hand mixer, whip all ingredients together in a large bowl until light and fluffy, approximately 5 minutes.

PUMPKIN KNOT DINNER ROLLS

Yields 2 dozen rolls

If you aren't a fan of pumpkin, don't let the pumpkin in these rolls scare you from trying them—they are so much more than just another seasonal fall treat. The pumpkin puree in this recipe does not infuse pumpkin flavor, but rather adds moisture, fiber, and sugar to classic dinner rolls, creating a soft, moist texture and a beautiful golden color. I like these rolls with poppy seeds sprinkled on top. They look perfect on a holiday dinner table. Serve with soft butter and jam or with Honey Butter (p. 163).

1 cup pumpkin puree

4 eggs, divided

1 cup warm milk

5 tablespoons plus 1 teaspoon butter, at room temperature

½ cup sugar

2 tablespoons instant yeast

1½ teaspoons salt

6 to 7 cups flour, divided

Canola oil

Poppy seeds

Additional butter, melted, for brushing

1. Preheat the oven to 350°F.

2. In a stand mixer, combine the pumpkin puree, 3 of the eggs, warm milk, butter, sugar, yeast, salt, and 1 cup of the flour. Gradually add the remaining 5 to 6 cups flour until the dough is tacky but not overly sticky and pulls away from the side of the mixing bowl. Continue to knead for a few more minutes. Drizzle in a little canola oil to help the dough release from the bowl.

3. Dump the dough onto a countertop greased with cooking spray.

4. Cut 2-ounce pieces of dough, using a kitchen scale to measure the weight. Using two hands, roll each piece of dough into a smooth rope, 8 to 9 inches long. Tie a loose knot with the dough, tucking the tails underneath the knot and pinching it all together on the underside. Repeat with the remaining dough, placing the dough knots about 3 inches apart on lightly greased baking sheets.

4. Place the knots in a warm area to rise for about 1 hour, or until puffed up. In a small bowl, whisk the remaining egg. Very carefully brush the knots with beaten egg, then sprinkle them with poppy seeds.

5. Bake at 350°F for 25 to 30 minutes, or until lightly golden. Remove from the oven and brush with melted butter.

JODY'S HOMEMADE BREAD

Yields 3 (1.5-pound) loaves

The scent of fresh-baked bread in my kitchen evokes precious memories of piano lesson days. As a young girl I took piano lessons with Miss Pedroja, and I vividly remember how her home always smelled of delicious, fresh-baked bread. While we sat at the piano in the front room, her mother was often in the kitchen baking bread. It felt warm, cozy, and safe. In that spirit, this is my go-to bread recipe. Your home will smell amazing while this bread bakes.

1. In a stand mixer fitted with a dough hook, mix together the ¾ cup flour, brown sugar, granulated sugar, cold water, boiling water, and canola oil. Add wheat flour and instant yeast and continue mixing. Then add 6 to 7 cups bread flour until the tackiness is equivalent to the back of a sticky note and pulls away from the bowl.

2. Drizzle in a little canola oil to help the dough release from the bowl. Dump the dough onto a lightly greased countertop. Divide into three 1½-pound portions (use a kitchen scale to get roughly equal weights). Shape into plain loaves, or follow the instructions for Cinnamon Swirl Bread (see sidebar on the next page). Place the dough in 8½ x 4½ x 2⅝-inch loaf pans lightly greased with cooking spray. Let rise for 1 hour, or until the loaves have risen about ½ inch over the top of the bread pans. While the dough is rising, preheat the oven to 350°F.

3. Bake the risen loaves at 350°F for 25 minutes. Cool for 10 minutes, then remove from pan. Brush with melted butter.

¾ cup all-purpose or bread flour

½ cup packed brown sugar

¼ cup granulated sugar

1⅔ cups cold water

1⅓ cups boiling water

¾ cup canola oil

2 cups wheat flour

2 tablespoons plus ¾ teaspoons instant yeast (3 small packets)

6 to 7 cups additional bread flour

Canola oil

Melted butter, for brushing

CINNAMON SWIRL BREAD

1 batch Jody's Homemade Bread (p. 167)

1 egg, beaten

½ cup granulated sugar

½ cup packed brown sugar

½ cup ground cinnamon

Melted butter, for brushing

1. Follow the recipe for Jody's Homemade Bread, but after dividing the dough into three equal portions, roll each portion into a long, narrow strip, about 18 x 6 inches. Brush with beaten egg.

2. In a small bowl, combine the granulated sugar, brown sugar, and cinnamon. Spread ¼ cup of the mixture over the brushed egg. Spread evenly with a small, angled spatula or the back of a spoon. Starting at the short end of the dough, begin rolling it up tightly, being careful to keep the rolled log in a 6- to 7-inch loaf as you roll it up. Pinch the seam well and roll it to the bottom of the loaf. Using a sharp paring knife, pierce five or six holes through the top of the loaf all the way to the bottom. This helps eliminate air pockets. Gently lift each loaf into a well-greased 8½ x 4½ x 2⅝-inch loaf pan and let rise in a warm location for 1 to 1½ hours, or until the loaves have risen about ½ inch over the top of the bread pans. While the dough is rising, pre-heat the oven to 350°F.

3. Bake risen loaves at 350°F for 25 to 30 minutes, or until the bread is moderately golden. Remove from the oven and immediately brush with melted butter. Allow to cool before storing in bags.

Tip: When making Cinnamon Swirl Bread, brush beaten egg on the bread dough before adding the cinnamon-sugar mixture, then roll up tightly. This will ensure nice layers that won't separate as easily.

FOUR-CHEESE GARLIC HERB ROLLS

Yields about 36 rolls

These savory rolls are stuffed with flavor—herbs, pesto, and a blend of four cheeses all packed within a homemade dough and rolled up in "cinnamon roll" fashion. The dough can be hand-kneaded the old-fashioned way, but it is super easy to prepare if you use a stand mixer with a dough hook.

1. In a large bowl or the bowl of a stand mixer, combine the warm water, ¾ cups plus 2 tablespoons of the canola oil, 5 cups of the flour, sugar, instant yeast, and salt. If using a stand mixer, turn the mixer on low speed until the ingredients are incorporated. Increase the speed to smooth the dough, or mix vigorously by hand.

2. Turn the mixer back to low. While mixing, slowly add the remaining 5 to 6 (or more) cups flour. I go entirely by looks. You do not want the dough to be dry and crumbly. (*Tip:* When the dough kneads together and mostly "cleans" the side of the bowl, you have added enough flour.) Knead at this speed for 3 to 4 minutes. Just before shutting off the mixer, drizzle in the remaining ¼ cup canola oil, then immediately shut off the mixer. This coats the dough so it is easy to handle and effortlessly slides out of the bowl. If you are not using a mixer, knead by hand for 3 to 4 minutes, adding canola oil at the very end.

3. Dump the dough onto a countertop lightly greased with cooking spray. Using a long serrated knife, cut the dough into three equal pieces. Roll each ball of dough into a rectangle, about 18 x 6 inches.

4. Using a small, angled spreader, spread the pesto very, very thinly over the dough (you want the pesto to be very sparse; it doesn't take much to give it a punch of flavor). Evenly sprinkle each sheet of dough with 3 cups of the shredded mozzarella/provolone blend, 2 cups of the shredded cheddar, and ¼ cup of the grated Parmesan cheese. Sprinkle Italian seasoning over the cheeses.

5. Beginning on the long side of the rectangle, tightly roll up the dough into a long log. Pinch the seams very tightly to prevent the log from unrolling. Rock and shape the log (seam side down) into a long, smooth log. It should be no more than 3 inches in diameter.

3¾ cups plus 2 tablespoons warm water (do not use hot water, as it will kill the yeast)

1 cup plus 2 tablespoons canola oil, divided

10 to 11 cups flour, divided

1 cup sugar

2 tablespoons instant yeast

1 tablespoon plus ¼ teaspoon salt

1 (6-ounce) jar pesto (refrigerate any remaining pesto for another use)

9 cups shredded mozzarella and provolone cheese blend, divided

6 cups shredded cheddar cheese, divided

¾ cup grated Parmesan cheese, divided, plus additional for sprinkling

Italian seasoning

¼ cup (½ stick) butter, melted

Garlic salt

6. Using a long serrated knife, cut 1 to 2 inches of dough off one end and discard. This helps ensure that you begin with a roll size that will remain consistent as you cut the log. Continue to slice 1-inch slices, or "rolls," supporting the roll with your other hand as you cut. The log will slice much better if you do not force a cut; rather, use a gentle, long sawing motion with the serrated knife. When you reach the last 1- to 2-inch portion of the dough log, stop and discard the remaining end. (Sometimes I choose to keep the discarded ends and arrange them in a separate small pan to bake alongside the rolls. They will taste wonderful, but they may not look as pretty as the other rolls.)

7. As you cut, place each roll into a greased 13 x 9-inch pan. Line up the rolls 4 x 3 to yield 12 rolls per pan. Repeat until all the prepared dough is cut into rolls and in the pans. Lightly cover the pans with plastic wrap and place them in a warm place to rise. This will take about 1½ hours. The dough will expand, and the sides should touch. While the rolls are rising, preheat the oven to 350°F.

8. Bake the risen rolls at 350°F for 25 to 30 minutes, or until the rolls are light golden brown and the dough is fully baked. Remove from the oven. While the rolls are hot, brush them heavily with the melted butter and sprinkle on additional Italian seasoning and grated Parmesan cheese. Add a light sprinkling of garlic salt. (The salt brings out the flavor!)

9. Serve warm with lasagna, spaghetti, or any other Italian dishes. Extra rolls can be frozen in the pans: Allow rolls to cool, seal the pans well, and freeze for up to 3 months. To serve, remove a pan from the freezer to thaw at room temperature for several hours. Cover the pan with aluminum foil and heat at 350°F for 15 to 20 minutes, or until the rolls are warm and the cheese is partially melted.

ROSEMARY SEA SALT
FOCACCIA BREAD

Yields 1 (18 x 13-inch) half-sheet pan

I experimented with this recipe years ago at The Homestead. It is a fun twist on bread, with its delightful crunch on the bottom crust and chewy texture on top. Loaded with oil, flavorful herbs, and coarse salt, this focaccia is a nice complement to any meal.

1 cup warm water

2 teaspoons extra-virgin olive oil

2 teaspoons honey

2⅔ cups flour

1 tablespoon instant yeast

1 teaspoon salt

Additional extra-virgin olive oil

Garlic powder

Dried rosemary

Italian seasoning

Coarse sea salt

1. Combine the warm water, olive oil, honey, flour, instant yeast, and salt in a stand mixer fitted with a dough hook. Knead for about 5 minutes, then remove the ball of dough from the bowl.

2. Grease an 18 x 13-inch half-sheet baking pan with cooking spray. Roll the dough directly on the sheet pan. (I use a small rolling pin or a mini dough roller.) Try to square the corners as much as possible. The dough will be ¼ inch thick (or less). Let it rise to about ½ inch, about 30 minutes. While the dough rises, preheat the oven to 450°F.

3. Using the handle of a wooden spoon (or something equivalent), push divot holes into, but not completely through, the risen dough. Do this about every inch across the whole pan.

4. Drizzle extra-virgin olive oil *very liberally* over the entire pan so that it settles into the divots and slightly pools on the dough (I use about 1½ cups oil). Use a pastry brush to spread the oil so that it covers the entire surface.

5. Sprinkle garlic powder, dried rosemary, Italian seasoning, and coarse sea salt over the dough. Go light on the sea salt; a little goes a long way.

6. Bake at 450°F for about 8 minutes, or until moderately golden. Remove from the oven and let it stand for 10 to 15 minutes. This will allow the oil to absorb into the bread, creating an amazing flavor and texture. Cut into 2-inch squares and enjoy!

FRENCH BREAD LOAVES

Yields 2 loaves

1. Combine the shortening, the 2 tablespoons sugar, and salt in a stand mixer bowl fitted with a dough hook. Add boiling water. Turn the mixer on low and stir until the sugar is dissolved and the mixture cools to lukewarm. Add 3 cups of the all-purpose flour, the whole wheat flour, instant yeast, and the ½ teaspoon sugar.

2. Grease an 18 x 13-inch half-sheet baking pan with cooking spray. Sprinkle cornmeal where the two loaves will be placed on the pan. Set aside.

3. Mix the dough until smooth. Gradually add the remaining 2½ to 3 cups all-purpose flour until the kneaded dough is smooth and elastic and cleans the side of the bowl. Drizzle in a little canola oil just before shutting off the mixer.

4. Divide the dough into two equal pieces and shape into long French-style loaves (about 12 inches long and 2 inches in diameter). Place the two loaves on the prepared baking pan on top of the cornmeal. Using a long serrated knife, make four to five quick, shallow, diagonal slits in the top of the bread.

5. Let the loaves rise until they are about doubled in size, 45 to 60 minutes. While the dough is rising, preheat the oven to 400°F. Brush risen loaves carefully with beaten egg. Bake at 400°F for 20 minutes, or until loaves are light golden.

6. For an extra-delicious treat, I like to slice the bread into ¾- to 1-inch slices and spread thick, soft butter on one side of each slice (I use ½ cup to ¾ cup butter—1 to 1½ sticks—for both loaves). Line the bread slices back into a loaf shape and wrap the whole loaf in heavy-duty aluminum foil. Repeat slicing and buttering with the second loaf—if you don't plan to eat it now, you can freeze it and serve it at another meal. Heat one or both loaves in the oven at 350°F for 10 to 15 minutes, or until heated through. If heating a loaf that has been frozen, make sure it is fully thawed before heating. This buttered, sliced bread also makes amazing French toast (see French Toast with Raspberry Sauce, p. 73).

2 tablespoons vegetable shortening

2 tablespoons plus ½ teaspoon sugar

2 teaspoons salt

2½ cups boiling water

5½ to 6 cups all-purpose flour, divided

1 cup whole wheat flour

4½ teaspoons instant yeast

Yellow or white cornmeal, for sprinkling

Canola oil

1 egg, beaten

Softened butter, for serving (optional)

FROSTED CINNAMON ROLLS

Yields 2 dozen rolls

I love to experiment with different ways to enjoy sweet rolls. My favorite—and the most popular—is the classic frosted cinnamon roll. I always think of my mom when I make her caramel pecan rolls, although as hard as I try, mine never turn out as perfect as hers. In the summertime, I love to serve a fruit version using blueberry or raspberry mash in place of the cinnamon swirl. I have the advantage of buying concentrated mashes from our local fudge company. They are packed with intense flavor and give the rolls a beautiful and flavorful swirl. Whether you go classic or try the fruit variant (p. 178), be sure to enjoy them with homemade cream cheese frosting spread over top of these rolls!

1. In a stand mixer fitted with a dough hook, beat together ½ cup of the flour, warm water, milk, shortening, 2 of the eggs, butter, potato flakes, sugar, yeast, and salt for a few minutes. Add the vanilla and the remaining 6 to 7 cups flour, kneading in just enough flour until the dough is soft and doesn't stick to the side of the bowl.

2. Just before stopping the mixer, drizzle in a little canola oil. Dump the soft dough onto a lightly greased countertop. Divide the dough in half. Roll each half into a long narrow rectangle, 6 to 7 inches wide.

3. In a small bowl, whisk the remaining egg. Brush the rolled sheets of dough with beaten egg, then sprinkle lightly with brown sugar and sprinkle heavily with cinnamon. Starting on the long side, roll up the dough tightly, creating a long log. Pinch the seam firmly into the log. Gently roll the log back and forth to smooth it out, leaving the seam on the bottom. Repeat with the other dough.

4. Cut about 1 inch off each end of each log to create a clean edge (discard these cut ends or make a mini roll baked in a separate pan). Using a long serrated knife, cut the log into 1-inch rolls. Place rolls in two lightly greased 13 x 9-inch pans, 12 rolls per pan (rows 4 x 3). Cover with greased plastic wrap and let rise in a warm location. This may take 1 to 1½ hours. The sides of the risen rolls should be touching. While the rolls are rising, preheat the oven to 350°F.

5. Bake the risen rolls at 350°F for 25 minutes, or until they are moderately golden. Cool to lukewarm and frost with Cream Cheese Frosting.

6. *To make Cream Cheese Frosting:* Beat together all the frosting ingredients with a hand mixer until smooth. Add milk 1 tablespoon at a time until the frosting reaches your desired consistency. Spread over the lukewarm sweet rolls.

6½ to 7 cups flour, divided

2 cups plus 1 tablespoon warm water

⅓ cup milk

⅔ cup vegetable shortening

3 eggs, divided

1 tablespoon butter, softened

⅔ cup instant potato flakes

⅔ cup sugar

1 tablespoon instant yeast

1½ teaspoons salt

½ teaspoon vanilla extract

Canola oil

Brown sugar

Ground cinnamon

Cream Cheese Frosting

3 ounces cream cheese, at room temperature

½ cup (1 stick) butter, at room temperature

4 cups powdered sugar

1 teaspoon vanilla extract

1 teaspoon almond extract

Several tablespoons milk

Tip: Frost these rolls when they are still *slightly* warm. This will relax the frosting just enough to lightly ooze into the layers. Be sure to completely cover the roll for superior presentation and ooey goodness in every bite. Before I frost these rolls, I use a small serrated knife to cut mostly through the outside edges of each roll. Precutting the rolls makes it easy to scoop and serve rolls at the table. When you add the frosting, the cut lines will not be visible.

CARAMEL PECAN ROLLS

½ cup (1 stick) butter

2 cups packed brown sugar

½ cup milk

2 cups chopped pecans

1. Melt the butter in a small saucepan, then add the brown sugar and milk. Heat and stir constantly with a rubber spatula until the mixture comes to a solid boil, then immediately remove from heat. Pour roughly even amounts of the hot mixture into two greased 13 x 9-inch pans. Sprinkle the chopped pecans evenly over the top of the caramel mixture.

2. Follow the instructions for Cinnamon Rolls (p. 176), but after cutting the log into rolls, place 12 rolls (rows 4 x 3) *on top* of the caramel mixture. Cover with greased plastic wrap and let rise in a warm location, 1 to 1½ hours. Bake in a preheated 350°F oven for 25 minutes, or until the rolls are moderately golden. Remove from the oven and let stand for 1 minute. Quickly invert the pan into another pan and scrape out the caramel pecan topping over the rolls. Cool and enjoy!

FROSTED BLUEBERRY OR RASPBERRY ROLLS

12 to 16 ounces blueberry or raspberry fruit mash

1. Follow the instructions for Cinnamon Rolls (p. 176), replacing the brushed beaten egg, brown sugar, and cinnamon with fruit mash. Spread the fruit mash very thinly over the sheeted dough with a small, angled spreader tool. (If you apply the fruit mash too thick, it will become messy and slide and ooze out as you try to roll up the dough.) Starting from the long end, roll up the sheeted dough and pinch the seams. Cut about 1 inch off the ends of the log to create a clean edge (discard these cut ends or make a mini roll baked in a separate pan). Using a long serrated knife, cut the logs into 1-inch slices.

2. Place 12 rolls (rows 4 x 3) into a lightly greased 13 x 9-inch pan. Cover with greased plastic wrap and let rise in a warm location. Bake in a preheated 350°F oven for 25 minutes, or until rolls are moderately golden. Cool to lukewarm and frost with Cream Cheese Frosting (p. 177).

PIZZA CRUST

Yields 2 (16-inch) pizza crusts

We occasionally like to order pizza on a busy night, but when I get the notion to make my own, this is the crust recipe I like to use. I also love to use it for Dessert Pizza Breadsticks (p. 288) and for Chicago Deep Dish Pizza (p. 239).

2¼ cups warm water

¼ teaspoon sugar

1 teaspoon salt

5 to 6 cups flour, divided

1 tablespoon instant yeast

1. Preheat the oven to 450°F.

2. In a stand mixer fitted with a dough hook, mix together the warm water, sugar, salt, and about half the flour. Add instant yeast. Mix until smooth. Continue adding flour, up to 6 cups *total*, until a soft dough is formed. Knead on low speed until smooth and elastic, about 10 minutes. Place in a greased large bowl, then flip the dough ball over so the entire ball is coated.

3. Divide the dough ball into two sections. Roll each ball into a 16-inch pizza crust. I like to roll my crusts directly onto a large seasoned pizza stone. I roll the crust completely to the stone edge. Let rise for 15 minutes.

4. Bake at 450°F for 5 to 6 minutes. Remove the crust from the oven and cover with your favorite pizza sauce and toppings.

5. Return the pizza to the oven at 450°F for about 10 minutes, or until the top is nice and golden and any cheese is melted. Pizza is also delicious baked on a pellet grill if you have one.

Note: These crusts freeze well. Prebake for 6 minutes, allow to cool, and wrap tightly to freeze for up to 3 months. To use a frozen crust, set it out at room temperature for about 2 hours, cover it with your favorite sauce and toppings, and finish baking in a preheated 450°F oven for 10 minutes.

MAIN DISHES

I was raised on a Kansas dairy farm and married an Indiana hog farmer, so we eat an abundance of beef and pork to support both. But we like chicken dishes too!

BEEF

Aunt Marilyn's Wiggles Casserole 184

Creamy Beef Stroganoff 187

Tater Tot Casserole 188

Lasagna 191

Goulash 192

Meat Loaf 195

Spaghetti Sauce 196

Taco-Filled Pasta Shells 199

Mom's Slow Cooker Pot Roast and
Quick Mashed Potatoes 200

Bacon-Wrapped Beef Patties 205

Montreal Marinated Grilled Steak 206

POULTRY

Bacon-Wrapped Caramelized
Chicken Tenders 209

Chicken or Beef Stir-Fry 210

Chicken Potpie 213

Chicken Tacos 214

Christmas Dinner Cornish Game Hen 217

Roasted Whole Chicken 218

Smoked Chicken Thighs with
White Barbecue Sauce 221

Swiss Chicken 222

Crispy Coated Baked Chicken 225

Mom's Chicken and Rice Casserole 226

PORK

Ham and Noodle Cheese Bake 229

Sausage and Potato Casserole 230

Barbecue Ribs 233

Herb Roasted Pork Loin
with Cilantro Cream Sauce 236

Chicago Deep Dish Pizza 239

Oven-Roasted Smoked Sausage and Potatoes 240

Italian Stromboli 243

Cheesy Brown Sugar Pork Chops 244

AUNT MARILYN'S WIGGLES CASSEROLE

Serves 8 to 10

When I married into the Bahler family, I was introduced to "Wiggles." This casserole dish was a favorite around their family dinner table. The recipe was passed down from dear Aunt Marilyn. We knew anything coming from her kitchen was special! Aunt Marilyn will always be remembered for her sweet disposition and the birthday cards that she faithfully hand-delivered to all the local extended family and friends. Each envelope was stuffed with a bag of M&M's (no matter our age!), and her beautiful handwriting addressed the special receiver—"Dear nephew Mike"—always underscored with a squiggly line.

1 pound ground beef

½ cup diced onion

1½ cups uncooked curly egg noodles

2 cups frozen peas

1 (10.5-ounce) can cream of mushroom soup

¼ cup milk

½ pound process cheese spread, sliced

1 (10.5-ounce) can tomato soup

¼ cup (½ stick) butter, melted

2 sleeves buttery crackers (I prefer Town House), crushed*

1. Preheat the oven to 350°F. Cook the ground beef and onion together. Drain and set aside. Cook the noodles according to package instructions just until al dente, then drain. Combine the cooked noodles, ground beef mixture, and peas. Spread this into a greased 13 x 9-inch pan.

2. In another small bowl, combine the cream of mushroom soup and milk. Pour this over the meat and noodles. Layer slices of process cheese spread, completely covering the top. Then spread the tomato soup over the cheese. Combine the melted butter and crushed cracker crumbs and sprinkle on top. Cover with more process cheese spread, if desired.

3. Bake, uncovered, at 350°F for 30 minutes, or until light golden and bubbly.

* Here's an easy and mess-free way to crush a sleeve of unopened crackers: Push inward from each end at the same time as hard as you can to compress the crackers. When you release pressure, you will find the crackers to be crushed. Open one end of the sleeve and dump them out.

CREAMY BEEF STROGANOFF

Serves 8 to 10

This comforting casserole is one of The Homestead's top sellers!

1. Preheat the oven to 350°F. Prepare the noodles according to package instructions in salted water just until barely tender, drain, and set aside. Do not overcook. Cook the ground beef and onion together, drain, and set aside.

2. In a large saucepan on low heat or in the microwave, heat the process cheese spread, soups, sour cream, milk, butter, garlic salt, and seasoned salt. Whisk together until the cheese spread is melted and the sauce is smooth.

3. When the sauce is melted, gently stir in the cooked and drained ground beef and noodles. Put in a greased 13 x 9-inch baking pan, or divide between two smaller pans and freeze one to bake later.

4. Bake, uncovered, at 350°F for 30 to 45 minutes until hot. For an extra crunch, sprinkle French fried onions on the top before the last 10 minutes of bake time.

7 ounces (4 cups) dry curly egg noodles

1 pound ground beef

¼ cup finely chopped onion

½ pound process cheese spread, cut into small cubes

1 (10.5-ounce) can cream of mushroom soup

1 (10.5-ounce) can cream of chicken soup

¾ cup sour cream

¾ cup milk

2 tablespoons (¼ stick) butter

½ teaspoon garlic salt

¼ teaspoon Shipshewana Happy Salt or another seasoned salt

French fried onions (optional)

TATER TOT CASSEROLE

Serves 10 to 12

This all-in-one casserole meal includes meat, potato, and vegetables. It is a good one to make ahead and keep in the freezer too.

2 pounds ground beef

1 onion, diced

1 (12-ounce) package frozen peas (do not thaw)

1 (10.5-ounce) can cream of chicken soup

4 cups shredded cheddar cheese

1 (32-ounce) package tater tots

Salt and pepper

1. Preheat the oven to 350°F.

2. Cook the beef and onion together. Drain, then spread in a greased 13 x 9-inch pan. Spread the frozen peas evenly over the ground beef. Using a small, angled spreader or the back of a spoon, spread the cream of chicken soup evenly over the peas. Spread the shredded cheese over everything. Line up the tater tots snugly across the top of the casserole.

3. Sprinkle with salt and pepper.

4. Bake, uncovered, at 350°F for 1 hour or longer. I like to bake it until the tater tots are golden and crunchy.

LASAGNA

Lasagna is another one of those dishes (like chili!) that everyone makes a little differently. There are so many versions! This is a basic lasagna that always works for me. I love the ease of oven-ready noodles.

1. Preheat the oven to 350°F. In a bowl, combine the cooked and drained beef with the onion, pasta sauce, garlic salt, oregano, basil, and pepper. In a separate bowl, combine the cottage cheese, 2 tablespoons grated Parmesan, and shredded cheese blend.

2. In a greased 13 x 9-inch deep-dish baking pan, layer in the following ingredients:
- A third of the meat sauce
- A layer of uncooked oven-ready lasagna noodles
- Half the cheese mixture
- A third of the meat sauce
- A layer of uncooked oven-ready lasagna noodles
- Remaining cheese mixture
- Remaining meat sauce

3. Top with a sprinkling of Parmesan cheese and Italian seasoning. Bake, uncovered, at 350°F for 1 hour, or until bubbly. Let it stand for 15 minutes before serving. This is delicious served with Four-Cheese Garlic Herb Rolls (p. 169).

2 pounds ground beef, cooked and drained

½ cup diced onion

1 (24-ounce) jar garlic pasta sauce (I prefer Bertolli Olive Oil & Garlic)

1¼ teaspoons garlic salt

1 teaspoon dried oregano

½ teaspoon dried basil

⅛ teaspoon pepper

1½ cups cottage cheese (4% small curd)

2 tablespoons grated Parmesan cheese plus additional for sprinkling

4 cups shredded mozzarella and provolone cheese blend

Oven-ready lasagna noodles (do not cook), enough to make two pan layers

Italian seasoning, for topping

GOULASH

Serves 6 to 8

Goulash evokes sweet childhood memories of when Mom made this dish. It is not fancy, but it is a delicious one-pan meal for busy nights!

1 pound ground beef

¼ cup diced onion

1 (14.5-ounce) can petite diced tomatoes (do not drain)

1 (10.5-ounce) can tomato soup

1¼ cups water

1 cup uncooked elbow macaroni

1 tablespoon Worcestershire sauce

1 tablespoon packed brown sugar

1 teaspoon garlic powder

½ teaspoon salt

⅛ teaspoon pepper

Italian seasoning, for topping

1. In a large nonstick skillet with a tight-fitting lid, cook the ground beef and diced onion together on medium-high heat until the beef is cooked through. Drain off excess drippings.

2. Add the remaining ingredients *except* the Italian seasoning to the skillet with the cooked beef. Stir together well and bring to a boil. When it boils, reduce the heat to low, put on the lid, and simmer for 20 minutes, or until the macaroni is tender. Remove the lid a couple of times during those 20 minutes to stir and make sure the mixture is not sticking to the pan. If it seems a little dry, you can add an additional ¼ to ½ cup water.

3. This can be served right out of the skillet at the table! Sprinkle Italian seasoning over the top before serving.

MEAT LOAF

Serves 6 to 8

We were raised on beef and always had an abundance of it in the freezer. Mom's meat loaf was a favorite that I tucked away in my personal recipe box. I like to serve meat loaf with cheesy potatoes. I did not include that as a separate recipe in this book because it's such a basic side dish: I peel, cut, and boil coarsely chopped potatoes until tender, drain, then make a cheesy white sauce with lots of Velveeta process cheese spread, garlic salt, and pepper. Stir the cheese sauce into the tender potatoes, and you have a simple side dish to go alongside your meat loaf!

1. Preheat the oven to 350°F. Using clean hands, mix together all the ingredients *except* the ½ cup ketchup. Place meat mixture into a greased 13 x 9-inch pan and press into a shallow loaf down the center of the pan—leaving about 1-inch margin on both long sides. Drizzle ketchup over the top of the loaf (or use my Meat Loaf Sauce, which is spread over top 30 minutes into the baking time—see sidebar).

2. Bake at 350°F for 1 hour. Remove from the oven. I like to cut the meat loaf in half and lift each half out with a flat spatula onto a serving plate. Cut into slices and serve with additional ketchup as desired.

2 pounds ground beef

½ chopped onion

¼ cup finely chopped green bell pepper

2 slices bread, cut in small pieces and soaked in ⅓ cup milk for 10 minutes— then *drain the milk*

1 egg

2 tablespoons prepared mustard

½ teaspoon garlic salt

⅛ teaspoon pepper

½ cup ketchup, plus additional for serving,

MEAT LOAF SAUCE

You can spread this sauce over the top in place of the ketchup. Let the meat loaf bake for 30 minutes before adding this sauce.

1 cup ketchup

¾ cup packed brown sugar

1 teaspoon garlic powder

½ teaspoon onion powder

½ teaspoon liquid smoke

Combine all the ingredients in a small saucepan and bring to a bubble, stirring with a flat spatula. Remove from heat and set aside. When the meat loaf has baked for 30 minutes, remove from the oven and spread this sauce over the top. Continue baking for the full hour.

SPAGHETTI SAUCE

Serves 4 to 6

I have used this spaghetti sauce for years, and it never fails. When I was a busy stay-at-home mom, I liked to multiply this recipe several times and freeze it in meal-size portions to be used later for a quick evening meal. I hope you enjoy it as much as we do!

1 pound ground beef, cooked and drained

1 onion, chopped

2 (14.5-ounce) cans diced tomatoes (do not drain)

1 (8-ounce) can tomato sauce

1 (6-ounce) can tomato paste

1 tablespoon packed brown sugar

2 teaspoons minced fresh garlic

2 teaspoons dried basil

2 teaspoons dried oregano

1 teaspoon salt

To serve

Hot, cooked spaghetti noodles

Shredded cheddar cheese or grated Parmesan cheese

Cook ground beef; drain. In a large pot on the stove, add the cooked ground beef and all remaining ingredients. Simmer together over low heat for about 30 minutes, stirring occasionally so it doesn't stick. Remove from heat and serve over hot cooked spaghetti noodles. Top with shredded cheddar cheese or freshly grated Parmesan cheese.

This is another dish that also pairs well with Four-Cheese Garlic Herb Rolls (p. 169).

Note: Before cooking spaghetti noodles, I like to break them up into about three pieces instead of boiling the long pieces. It's much easier to eat, but if you like the experience of twisting long spaghetti with a fork, that is up to you. You can also find half-length spaghetti noodles in most grocery stores.

TACO-FILLED PASTA SHELLS

Yields 18 stuffed shells

This dish is a nice twist on traditional tacos. It is full of flavor and always a favorite! I like to make this full recipe, but I don't use all the shells at once. With only two of us at home, it works great to use half for our dinner and then freeze the remaining shells on a baking sheet (individually quick frozen). After they are frozen, I pop them off and store them in a resealable plastic freezer bag. They are easy to pull out and thaw for another meal—most of the work is done!

1. Preheat the oven to 350°F. Cook the ground beef and drain. Prepare the seasoning packets as directed on the package and add to the ground beef. Add the cream cheese and stir until the cheese is melted and creamy. Set aside to cool.

2. Boil the jumbo pasta shells just until tender. Drain, then toss the shells with butter until melted. Stuff each shell with the meat mixture. If making any shells to freeze for later use, they can now be frozen.

3. Spread the salsa into a greased 13 x 9-inch baking dish. Top with the stuffed shells and drizzle with taco sauce. Cover with aluminum foil and bake at 350°F for 30 minutes. Uncover and sprinkle with cheddar and Monterey Jack cheese and crushed chips. Bake for another 15 minutes. Serve at the table with sour cream and diced green onions.

3 pounds ground beef

3 (1-ounce) packets mild taco seasoning

1½ (8-ounce) blocks cream cheese, at room temperature

18 uncooked jumbo pasta shells (I usually cook a few more in case some break and fall apart)

6 tablespoons (¾ stick) butter

1½ cups mild salsa

1½ cups mild taco sauce

2 cups shredded cheddar cheese

2 cups shredded Monterey Jack cheese

3 cups crushed nacho cheese tortilla chips

1½ cups sour cream

4 green onions, diced

MOM'S SLOW COOKER POT ROAST AND QUICK MASHED POTATOES

Serves 10 to 12

My mom's pot roast is a classic, and it oozes comfort when served over a mound of buttery mashed potatoes or wide, buttered noodles. It creates its own gravy in the slow cooker. Super easy, and so delicious!

1 (2- to 3-pound) boneless beef roast

2 (10.5-ounce) cans cream of mushroom soup

⅓ cup sherry cooking wine

1 (1-ounce) packet dry onion soup mix

½ teaspoon garlic salt

¼ teaspoon pepper

1. Place the roast in a large, well-greased slow cooker. Whisk the remaining ingredients together in a small bowl and pour this mixture over the roast. Place the lid on the slow cooker and cook on high for 7 to 8 hours, or until the roast is very tender. Remove the roast and gravy from the slow cooker and put it in a serving pan for the table.

QUICK MASHED POTATOES

These are my everyday mashed potatoes—super easy and quick, but buttery and delicious.

4 to 5 russet potatoes, peeled and coarsely chopped

½ cup (1 stick) butter

½ teaspoon garlic salt

¼ teaspoon pepper

Milk (optional)

Place the potatoes in a pot and cover with water. Bring the water to a boil, then reduce the heat and let the potatoes lightly cook for 20 to 25 minutes. Do not let the pot boil dry! When the potatoes are tender, remove from heat and drain the water. Immediately add the butter, garlic salt, and pepper.

While the potatoes are still hot, whip with an electric hand beater until smooth and fluffy. If they are still a little stiff, you can drizzle in a tiny bit of milk, beating well. These are amazing served with Mom's Slow Cooker Pot Roast over the top.

man shall not live by bread alone, but by every word that proceedeth out of the mouth of God.

MATTHEW 4:4

BACON-WRAPPED BEEF PATTIES

Serves 8 to 10

These are a unique and delicious version of burgers. We love them smoked on our pellet grill. Remove the wooden picks before serving either on a bun or on their own.

1. Preheat the grill to medium-high heat.

2. Combine all the ingredients *except* the bacon strips, mixing well. Divide into 8 to 10 evenly sized balls. Shape each ball into a beef patty. Wrap each patty with a slice of raw bacon and secure well with a wooden pick along the side of the patty.

3. Place patties on the preheated grill and cook until the centers are done to your preference and the bacon around the burger is cooked. Be careful not to overcook or char the meat.

4. Remove from the grill and enjoy!

2 pounds ground beef

⅔ cup diced onion

1 cup shredded cheddar cheese

2 tablespoons grated Parmesan cheese

2 eggs

¼ cup ketchup

2 tablespoons Worcestershire sauce (shake well before measuring)

1 teaspoon salt

¼ teaspoon pepper

1 pound uncooked bacon strips

MONTREAL MARINATED GRILLED STEAK

Serves 2 to 3

Steak is a special treat, and we think that a good home-grilled steak far surpasses any steakhouse steak (although we enjoy plenty of those, too).

2 to 3 steaks of choice (preferred cuts are ribeye, strip steak, or filet mignon)*

Marinade

¼ cup canola oil

¼ cup water

2 tablespoons red wine vinegar

2 tablespoons Montreal steak seasoning

Steak butter

½ cup (1 stick) butter

1 teaspoon Montreal steak seasoning

1 teaspoon dried parsley

¼ teaspoon garlic powder

¼ teaspoon Worcestershire sauce

¼ teaspoon canola oil

1. Copiously poke both sides of the steaks with a fork to ensure great marinading results. Whisk the marinade ingredients together until well combined. Pour this mixture over the poked steaks. Flip the steaks to cover them all over with the marinade. Cover the marinated steaks with plastic wrap and refrigerate for 3 to 6 hours. I like to flip the steaks once during the marinating time.

2. While the steaks are marinating, prepare the steak butter: Melt the butter in a small saucepan over low heat. Whisk in the remaining ingredients. Set aside to use after grilling the steaks.

3. Place marinated steaks on a preheated grill, about 375°F, and grill until the centers are medium pink. Flip once while grilling. The internal temperature should be 140 to 150°F. Remove from the grill and immediately brush the steaks liberally with soft or melted steak butter. I like to dip my steak bites in Heinz 57 Sauce, but a good steak doesn't really need it.

* **Note:** The ultimate steak experience is Wagyu beef, from a Japanese descendant cattle. Wagyu is an expensive steak cut with intense marbling, which creates a luxurious, buttery tenderness.

There are several tips to cooking an amazing steak:
- Marinate the steak 3 to 6 hours before grilling.
- Do not overcook. Even after removing from the grill, the steak will continue to cook for a minute or two. I remove it from the heat when the steak still has a little soft pink in the center (a meat thermometer placed in the center should read 140°F to 150°F). Overcooking will result in tough steak.
- Baste the hot grilled steak with a good steak butter and let it melt into the meat. This enhances the flavor!

BACON-WRAPPED CARAMELIZED CHICKEN TENDERS

Serves 8 to 10

We like to serve this chicken over buttered rice.

1. Preheat the oven to 350°F. Stir the seasoned salt, onion powder, garlic powder, Italian seasoning, and pepper together and sprinkle the mixture all over the chicken tenders. Wrap each seasoned chicken tender with a bacon strip. Put wrapped chicken strips in a greased baking pan.

2. Sprinkle the brown sugar over the chicken and press it into the chicken to pack it in.

3. Bake at 350°F for 25 to 30 minutes, or until the chicken is cooked through and the bacon is crisp. If needed, you can turn the oven to broil for a few minutes to crisp the bacon.

2 teaspoons Shipshewana Happy Salt or another seasoned salt

2 teaspoons onion powder

2 teaspoons garlic powder

1 teaspoon Italian seasoning

1 teaspoon pepper

20 uncooked chicken tenders

20 slices uncooked bacon

1⅓ cups packed brown sugar

CHICKEN OR BEEF STIR-FRY

Serves 8 to 10

When the girls were growing up, this was a frequently requested favorite around our family table. Almost any variation of meat and vegetables can be used to create a dish suitable for your family. You may use either a combination of frozen stir-fry veggies plus a can of water chestnuts or a variety of freshly cut vegetables. See the sidebar for some suggested combinations.

1. *To prepare chicken:* Place the chicken in single layer on an aluminum foil–lined and greased baking sheet (easy cleanup!). Bake at 350°F for 1 hour. Allow to cool, then cut chicken into ¼-inch strips. Set aside.

To prepare steak: Cut the raw steaks into ¼-inch strips. (*Tip:* I prefer to cut the steaks when they are still partially frozen. This allows for neatly cut strips, and it is much easier to cut through the meat fibers if partially frozen.) Set aside.

2. Whisk together the stir-fry sauce ingredients; set aside.

3. Add canola oil to a large skillet and heat gently over medium heat for about 2 minutes.

4. *If using chicken:* Add cooked chicken slices to the oil in the skillet, and lightly cook and stir for about 1 minute.

If using steak: Add raw steak slices to the oil in the skillet and cook for 4 to 5 minutes, stirring often, until steak is browned or lightly golden. Turn heat to low and cover the skillet. Let the steak simmer for 1 to 2 minutes.

5. Add the frozen vegetables and water chestnuts or the fresh cut vegetables to the skillet. Immediately pour the prepared stir-fry sauce over the vegetables and put the lid on to steam the skillet contents. Steam with the lid on for 1 to 2 minutes over medium heat. Then remove the lid, stir well, and continue to cook, uncovered, until the vegetables are cooked to a desired tenderness, usually no more than 10 minutes.

6. Serve over hot, buttered rice.

2 pounds boneless chicken breasts, or 2 large sirloin or flat iron steaks

Stir-fry sauce

1 (0.74-ounce) packet Sun-Bird Stir-Fry Seasoning Mix or a similar mix of your choice

2 tablespoons soy sauce

½ cup water

For stir-fry

2 tablespoons canola oil

1 pound frozen mixed vegetables of your choice (no need to thaw) plus 1 (8-ounce) can water chestnuts (drain well) *or* 1 to 1½ pounds of your favorite fresh vegetables, chopped

Our family loves steak, and if I use my own vegetables, there are a few variations I like to use.

BEEF AND BROCCOLI STIR-FRY

1 head fresh broccoli, coarsely chopped

2 ribs celery, chopped

1 whole yellow onion, chopped

1 (8-ounce) can sliced water chestnuts, drained well

PEPPER STEAK STIR-FRY

2 large green bell peppers, chopped

2 ribs celery, chopped

1 whole yellow onion, chopped

1 (8-ounce) can sliced water chestnuts, drained well

CHICKEN POTPIE

Serves 6 to 8

Chicken Potpie is an all-in-one comfort meal, especially in the winter. To simplify the preparation, you can use prepared pie dough. If you want to make it from scratch, see my recipe for Flaky Pie Crust (p. 272). This recipe also calls for meat from a cooked rotisserie chicken; to save time, you might purchase one from your local grocery store.

1. Preheat the oven to 350°F. Prepare the unbaked pie crusts, one for the bottom and one for the top. Place the bottom crust in a lightly greased 9-inch pie pan.

2. In a large microwave-safe bowl, whisk together the evaporated milk, milk, melted butter, Thermflo, chicken bouillon, hot sauce, pepper, and garlic salt. Heat in the microwave, whisking occasionally, until thickened. When this mixture is thickened, stir in the shredded chicken, cubed hash browns, mixed vegetables, and peas. Spread this mixture into the bottom pie crust. Place the top crust over the filling. Crimp the edges of the crust together and cut slits across the top to allow steam to escape.

3. Brush the top crust very lightly with milk and sprinkle with dried parsley. Bake at 350°F for 1 hour, or until the filling bubbles up and the crust is golden. It is best to let the potpie stand for 15 to 20 minutes before serving.

2 (9-inch) pie crusts, one for the bottom and one for the top

1 (5-ounce) can evaporated milk

1 cup milk plus additional for brushing

4 tablespoons butter, melted

3 tablespoons Thermflo

1 tablespoon granulated chicken bouillon

2 drops hot sauce

¼ teaspoon pepper

⅛ teaspoon garlic salt

1 cooked rotisserie chicken, skinned, deboned, and shredded (you'll want about 3 cups meat)

1 cup cubed frozen hash browns

1 cup frozen mixed vegetables

½ cup frozen peas

Dried parsley, for sprinkling

CHICKEN TACOS

Serves 6 to 8

We eat a lot of beef, but this shredded chicken version of tacos is a nice change from the traditional preparation.

4 large boneless, skinless chicken breasts (about 2 pounds)

1 cup chicken broth

1 teaspoon garlic powder

½ teaspoon ground cumin

½ teaspoon onion salt

½ teaspoon salt

½ teaspoon pepper

Tortillas (hard or soft)

Toppings, as desired (see suggestions in point 2)

1. Place the chicken breasts in the bottom of a greased slow cooker. Cover with chicken broth and all the seasonings. Cover and cook on low for 7 to 8 hours. Remove the chicken from the slow cooker and shred it with a fork. Drizzle with some of the juices from the slow cooker.

2. Serve the shredded chicken with soft or hard tortilla shells, according to your preference. Build your own taco with your favorite toppings. We love to add the following options:

- Shredded lettuce
- Diced tomatoes or pico de gallo
- Sweet corn
- Green onion
- Shredded Monterey Jack cheese
- Guacamole (see recipe on p. 33)
- Sour cream (thinned with a little water)
- Freshly chopped cilantro
- Freshly squeezed lime

CHRISTMAS DINNER CORNISH GAME HEN

Serves 6

When the girls were about high school age, I started a tradition of serving Cornish game hen every year for Christmas dinner. It was always a fun treat, and they looked so nice and festive sitting on everyone's plate. Now that we have precious little people around the table and our numbers are growing, we have ventured away from the Cornish hen. However, this will always be a fun and delicious treat when we decide to try it again!

1. Check inside the hens and remove any giblets. Rinse the Cornish hens under cold running water, inside and out. Dry the hens thoroughly with a paper towel. For aesthetics, I like to tuck the wings and tie the legs together with butcher string.

2. Generously rub the outside of each hen with 1 tablespoon of softened butter. Season the hen with chicken rub and dried rosemary. Stuff a sprig of fresh rosemary inside the cavity of each hen.

3. Heat the wood pellet grill to 375°F. Roast the hens directly on the smoker for about 1 hour, or until the internal temperature of the thigh is 165°F. If you do not have a pellet grill, the hen can be roasted, uncovered, in the oven, with delicious results. Time and temperature will be the same as the pellet grill.

4. Remove hens from the grill or oven. Transfer them to individual plates and set one at each place setting at the table. Garnish with additional fresh rosemary, if desired.

6 Cornish game hens

6 tablespoons (¾ stick) butter, softened

Chicken rub (I prefer Traeger Chicken Rub)

Dried rosemary

6 springs fresh rosemary plus additional for garnish

Note: These are very cute and fun to eat, but they are messy! We always said two people could share one hen, but we never did. It was the novelty of having your own personal hen to eat that made it such a treat.

ROASTED WHOLE CHICKEN

Serves 4

Serving a whole chicken at the table can be a little awkward, but it is so delicious that it's worth it. Another way to eat this chicken is to remove and shred all the meat from the chicken and use it in soups and casseroles (including Chicken Potpie, p. 213). The meat is so tender and has a great flavor.

1 whole chicken

¾ cup (1½ sticks) butter, at room temperature

½ teaspoon lemon juice

4 sprigs fresh rosemary (2 chopped, 2 whole)

1 lemon, halved

Salt and pepper

1. Preheat the oven to 400°F.

2. Remove any giblet pieces from inside the chicken, rinse, and pat dry.

3. In a separate bowl, combine the softened butter, lemon juice, and the chopped sprigs of fresh rosemary.

4. Line a baking sheet with heavy-duty aluminum foil, spray it with cooking spray, and lay the patted-dry chicken on the foil, breast side up. Using clean hands, spread the soft butter mixture over the entire chicken, including inside the cavity as much as possible. I also try to lift the skin and spread butter under it as well.

5. Stuff the lemon halves and the two remaining sprigs of rosemary inside the cavity of the bird. Sprinkle salt and pepper over the whole chicken.

6. Place the chicken into the oven and roast it at 400°F for 75 minutes, or until a thermometer inserted in the meat reads 165°F. The skin should be deep golden brown, and the juices should be hot and sizzling.

SMOKED CHICKEN THIGHS WITH WHITE BARBECUE SAUCE

Serves 25

Our Homestead catering menu offers these smoked boneless chicken thighs. They make a lovely combination paired with our White Barbecue Sauce.

This recipe works well for a group and can be prepared ahead—I smoked a large amount of this chicken several days before a church dinner. I then arranged the smoked chicken in a well-greased electric roaster pan with 1 cup of water and refrigerated it until the day of the meal. On the morning of the gathering, I set the pan of chicken out at room temperature, then heated it on low/medium heat for a couple of hours before serving the midafternoon meal. We served it alongside the White Barbecue Sauce. This dish received many rave reviews regarding the juicy, flavorful chicken and the complementary White Barbecue Sauce.

1. *To make Chicken Rub:* Combine all the seasoning ingredients. This will make about 1½ cups and is handy to keep in the cupboard for other uses if you don't use all of it in this recipe.

2. Put the chicken thighs in a large bowl and add 1 cup rub (or more, if preferred). Mix it all together well with clean hands. I have found this the easiest way to distribute the seasoning.

3. Smoke on a smoker grill at 250°F for 40 to 45 minutes, or until the internal temperature of the chicken pieces is 165°F to 170°F. I don't flip them.

4. *To make White Barbecue Sauce:* Mix all the ingredients together. I prefer to make this 1 or 2 days ahead, which allows the sauce flavors to blend.

40 boneless, skinless chicken thighs (about 8 pounds)

Chicken Rub

⅓ cup packed brown sugar

⅓ cup granulated sugar

⅓ cup salt

4 teaspoons celery salt

4 teaspoons Lawry's or another seasoned salt

1 tablespoon Hungarian paprika

1 tablespoon chili powder

¾ teaspoon pepper

⅛ teaspoon garlic powder

⅛ teaspoon granulated onion

White Barbecue Sauce

1 cup sour cream

1 cup mayonnaise

2 tablespoons plus 2 teaspoons apple cider vinegar

2 tablespoons prepared horseradish

¾ teaspoon minced garlic

½ teaspoon lemon juice

⅛ teaspoon Worcestershire sauce

1 teaspoon pepper

¾ teaspoon sugar

¼ teaspoon salt

SWISS CHICKEN

Serves 6

You will enjoy the ease of this dish! It looks fancy, and it tastes even better.

6 boneless chicken breasts (about 2½ pounds)

6 slices Swiss cheese

1 (10.5-ounce) can cream of chicken soup

3 tablespoons white cooking wine

½ cup (1 stick) butter

1 (6-ounce) box chicken stuffing (I prefer Stove Top brand)

1. Preheat the oven to 350°F.

2. Lay chicken breasts in a greased 13 x 9-inch baking pan. Lay one slice of Swiss cheese over the top of each breast. Whisk together the soup and cooking wine and spread evenly over the chicken.

3. In a bowl, melt butter, then add stuffing. Stir until well combined. Spread this buttered stuffing evenly over the chicken in the pan.

4. Bake at 350°F for 45 to 60 minutes, or until the stuffing is golden brown and the chicken breasts are tender. Serve with rice, if desired.

CRISPY COATED BAKED CHICKEN

Serves 6

You could use chicken breasts in place of chicken tenders, but we like the smaller pieces . . . and besides, they have more surface area for the crunch! These are delicious dipped in ranch or barbecue sauce.

1. Preheat the oven to 350°F. Line a baking sheet with aluminum foil, grease it with cooking spray, and set aside.

2. Pat the chicken tenders dry with paper towel and set aside.

3. Place the cornflakes in a gallon-size resealable plastic bag, remove the air, and crush with a rolling pin until you have fine crumbs. Place the crumbs in a shallow pan or bowl.

4. Beat the egg and milk together. Beat in the flour, garlic powder, garlic salt, parsley, and pepper, mixing until smooth. Dip the chicken tenders in the batter, then completely coat them in the cornflake crumbs.

5. Place the coated chicken tenders on the foil-lined pan. Drizzle with melted butter. Bake, uncovered, at 350°F for 30 to 45 minutes, or until the chicken is tender and juices are clear. Do not cover the pan or turn the chicken while you are baking.

12 uncooked chicken tenders (about 1½ pounds)

7 cups cornflakes cereal (will yield about 1¾ cups crushed)

1 egg

1 cup milk

½ cup flour

½ teaspoon garlic powder

½ teaspoon garlic salt

½ teaspoon dried parsley

¼ teaspoon pepper

Melted butter, for drizzling

MOM'S CHICKEN AND RICE CASSEROLE

Serves 6 to 8

This casserole comes together so easily. My mom made it regularly while we were growing up, so it has lots of fond memories of days gone by when my siblings and I were seated around the table with Dad and Mom. Mom's simple meals had a way of making everything feel special. I loved this dish so much that, years ago, I slipped this recipe into my personal recipe box and started making it frequently for my own family.

2 tablespoons (¼ stick) butter, melted

1 tablespoon granulated chicken bouillon dissolved in 2 cups boiling water

2 (6-ounce) boxes Ben's Original Long Grain & Wild Rice Original Recipe (do not cook)

1 tablespoon seasoning from the packet in the box of rice

1 (10.5-ounce) can cream of chicken soup

1 (10.5-ounce) can cream of mushroom soup

12 boneless, skinless chicken thighs

1. Preheat the oven to 325°F.

2. Whisk together all the ingredients *except* the chicken. Spread 1½ cups mixture in the bottom of a greased 13 x 9-inch baking pan. Arrange the chicken thighs over the creamy rice mixture. Cover the thighs with the remaining rice mixture. Sprinkle with freshly ground pepper.

3. Bake, uncovered, at 325°F for 2 hours.

HAM AND NOODLE CHEESE BAKE

Serves 6

This was always a good dish to make when the girls were young. They loved it, and any picky eaters you know probably will, too.

1. Preheat the oven to 325°F.

2. Cook the macaroni just until tender. Drain and move to a large bowl. Add butter and toss with hot macaroni until butter is melted. Add remaining ingredients and mix well.

3. Pour the mixture into a greased 2-quart pan. Bake, uncovered, at 325°F for 45 to 60 minutes, or until the center is set. I like to stir partway through baking to ensure that the egg-based mixture cooks evenly and thoroughly.

1 cup elbow macaroni

¼ cup (½ stick) butter, cut into pieces

1 cup soft breadcrumbs (I put 3 to 4 bread slices in the blender and pulse it to make fine crumbs)

2 cups shredded cheddar cheese

2 cups chopped shaved ham

3 eggs, beaten well

1½ cups milk

1 tablespoon dried onion

1 tablespoon parsley flakes

¼ teaspoon salt

⅛ teaspoon pepper

SAUSAGE AND POTATO CASSEROLE

Serves 5 to 6

Since Mike raises hogs, we have an abundance of sausage in the freezer. This is one of my favorite casseroles. It is full of flavor, and the combination of sausage, potatoes, and cheese is so comforting. The French fried onions on the top add the perfect crunch. This is a delicious meal in the fall, and we like to serve it with Autumn Baked Apples (p. 113) and a loaf of home-made bread.

1 pound country sausage, cooked and drained

4 cups peeled and cubed potatoes

½ cup chopped onion

3 cups shredded cheddar cheese

1 (10.5-ounce) can cream of mushroom soup

¾ cup milk

¼ teaspoon pepper

¼ teaspoon salt

1 (6-ounce) package French fried onions

1. Preheat the oven to 350°F.

2. Mix all the ingredients *except* the French fried onions together in a large bowl. Pour the mixture into a greased 1½- to 2-quart baking dish.

3. Cover tightly with aluminum foil and bake at 350°F for 75 minutes. Then remove the aluminum foil and spread the French fried onions over the top of the casserole. Continue to bake, uncovered, for another 5 to 10 minutes, or until the onions are lightly toasted.

BARBECUE RIBS

Serves 6 to 8

I like to use boneless country-style ribs. They tend to be meatier than other cuts of ribs, and with their beautiful fat marbling creates a flavorful, tender piece of meat. But feel free to use any type of rib in this recipe.

1. Preheat the oven to 325°F. Combine all the sauce ingredients in a saucepan. Heat on low heat, stirring constantly, until the sugar is dissolved and the butter is melted—but do not let it boil. Set it aside. The sauce can also be refrigerated at this point.

2. Sear the ribs in a skillet in the canola oil, just long enough to brown them, about 2 minutes per side. You can also grill them just long enough to brown and gain grill marks. Remove them from the heat and heavily baste them on all sides with the barbecue sauce, then line them up in a deep pan. Drizzle a little more barbecue sauce over top, if desired.

3. Cover the pan tightly with aluminum foil. Bake at 325°F for 2 hours, or until the ribs are fork-tender. Carefully remove the ribs from the pan and put them on a serving platter or in a clean pan. Just before serving, drizzle diagonally with additional fresh sauce.

Barbecue Sauce

2½ cups packed brown sugar

1 (20-ounce) bottle ketchup (I prefer Heinz for its thick texture and rich color)

¼ cup (½ stick) butter

2 tablespoons plus 2 teaspoons white vinegar

1 tablespoon molasses

1 teaspoon Worcestershire sauce

¼ teaspoon liquid smoke

½ teaspoon garlic powder

8 to 10 boneless country-style ribs

2 tablespoons canola oil

behold,
I stand at
the door and
knock: if any
man hear my
voice, and
open the door,
I will come
in to him, and
will sup with
him, and he
with me.

REVELATION 3:20

HERB ROASTED PORK LOIN WITH CILANTRO CREAM SAUCE

Serves 20 to 24

This dish is so pretty that guests will think you spent all day in the kitchen, when in fact, this goes together in a snap.

1 uncooked pork loin

½ cup (1 stick) butter, cubed

1 (1-ounce) packet dry onion soup mix

2 tablespoons dried parsley

2 teaspoons Lawry's or another seasoned salt

2 teaspoons garlic salt

Cilantro Cream Sauce

4 ounces cream cheese, at room temperature

1 teaspoon sour cream

½ bunch fresh cilantro, finely chopped

¼ cup salsa verde

1 teaspoon freshly squeezed lime juice

1 teaspoon garlic powder

½ teaspoon celery salt

½ teaspoon pepper

¼ teaspoon ground cumin

1. Preheat the oven to 400°F. Arrange the loin in a lightly greased pan. For ease of baking, I like to cut the loin in half; it fits in the pan better. Place cubes of butter all over the loin. Combine the dry onion soup mix with the dried parsley, seasoned salt, and garlic salt, then sprinkle evenly over the loin.

2. Bake, uncovered, at 400°F for 20 minutes. Then reduce the temperature to 350°F and cover the pan tightly with aluminum foil. Bake another 1 to 1½ hours, or until a thermometer inserted in the loin reads 145°F. Be careful that the temperature doesn't go higher, so watch closely. Remove the loin from the oven and let it stand for 30 minutes.

3. After 30 minutes, move the cooked loin to a cutting board. Using an electric knife, cut thin ¼-inch slices and stagger them in a neat line in clean, greased baking dish. Drizzle any remaining juice from the pan over the sliced loin. Serve immediately, or refrigerate to reheat and serve later. This also freezes well. To reheat, put it in the oven at 350°F for 30 minutes, or just until hot. Do not overcook. Serve with Cilantro Cream Sauce as desired.

4. *To make Cilantro Cream Sauce:* Blend all the sauce ingredients together in a blender until smooth and creamy. Refrigerate until ready to serve alongside the roasted pork loin.

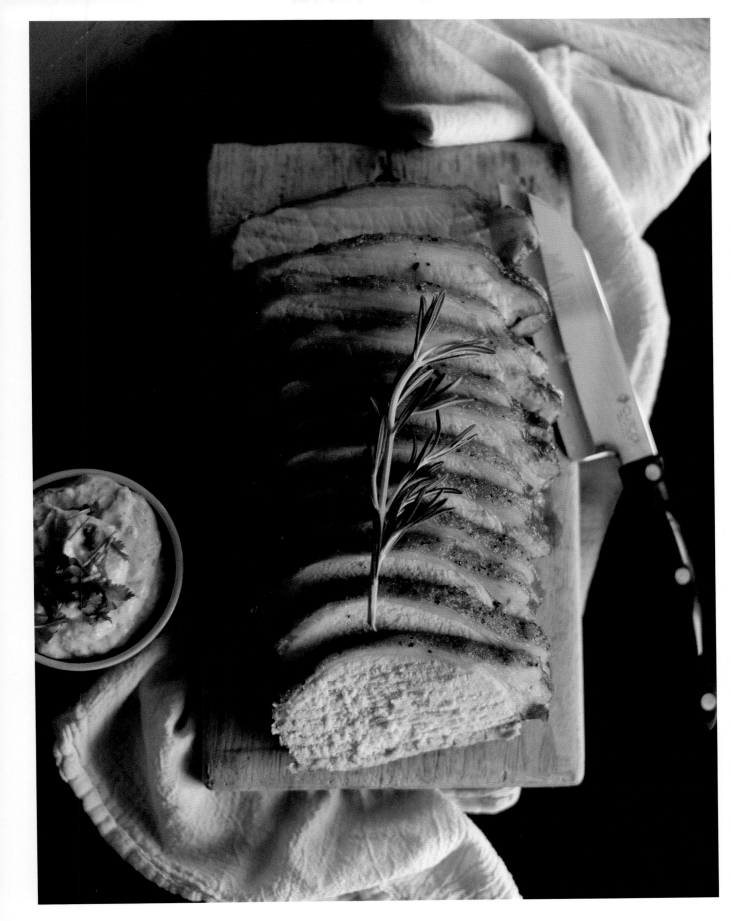

CHICAGO DEEP DISH PIZZA

Serves 8 to 10

Loaded with cheese and flavorful sausage, each slice is very filling. I set the frozen dough out in the morning, and it is ready to finish and bake for dinner when I get home. To save time later, you can cook the sausage and sauté the mushroom-and-tomato mixture ahead of time. Refrigerate both until it is time to assemble the pizza. This helps it come together in a hurry.

1. *If using frozen dough:* Place the frozen dough in a greased 13 x 9-inch pan. Cover lightly with plastic wrap greased with cooking spray and let it stand on the counter at room temperature for 6 to 8 hours. It will thaw and rise. Once the dough has risen, press the dough in the pan completely to the edges and slightly up the sides as best as you can.

If using freshly prepared dough: Prepare the dough in the pan as directed above. Because the dough does not need to thaw, the rising time will be shorter—about 1 to 1½ hours.

2. Preheat the oven to 350°F. Spread the cooked and drained sausage over the dough, then spread evenly with the shredded cheese.

3. In a skillet, cook and stir the mushrooms, onion, and oil together for a few minutes. Add the drained tomatoes, oregano, salt, and garlic powder and stir well. Spread this mixture over the shredded cheese.

4. Sprinkle with grated Parmesan cheese. Bake at 350°F for 25 to 35 minutes, or until crust is golden, being careful not to let it burn. Serve immediately.

1 pound frozen bread dough or 1 pound Pizza Crust dough (p. 180)

1 pound Italian or country sausage, cooked and drained

3 cups shredded mozzarella and provolone cheese blend

1 (8-ounce) can sliced mushrooms, drained

1 cup diced onion

2 teaspoons olive oil

1 (28-ounce) can petite diced tomatoes, drained

¾ teaspoon dried oregano

½ teaspoon salt

¼ teaspoon garlic powder

½ cup grated Parmesan cheese

OVEN-ROASTED SMOKED SAUSAGE AND POTATOES

Serves 4 to 5

Dishes like this one are easy to toss together, and most everyone loves the combination of smoky sausage and cheesy potatoes. It pairs well with partially frozen Chunky Applesauce (p. 110) on a crisp autumn day. Or serve alongside fresh-baked Pumpkin Chocolate Chip Muffins (p. 157).

1 (14- to 16-ounce) package smoked sausage loop (or kielbasa), sliced ½-inch thick at an angle (you do not need to cook this first)

5 large potatoes, peeled and chopped into ½-inch pieces*

1 large onion, chopped

2 tablespoons canola oil

Salt and pepper

Garlic salt

2 cups shredded cheddar cheese

1. Preheat the oven to 400°F.

2. Line a baking sheet with heavy-duty aluminum foil. Grease the foil with cooking spray.

3. In a large bowl, toss together the sausage, potatoes, and onion for even distribution. Stir in the canola oil. Season as desired with salt and pepper, mixing well. Spread this mixture out on the foil-covered baking sheet. Sprinkle lightly with garlic salt.

4. Roast at 400°F for 45 to 60 minutes, or until the potatoes are golden and tender. I like to stir the contents halfway through baking.

5. When the potatoes are tender and golden, remove the pan from the oven. Sprinkle shredded cheddar cheese over top. Put the pan back in the oven for 1 to 2 minutes to melt the cheese.

* ***Tip:*** Always keep peeled potatoes covered in water to prevent them from turning dark. When you are ready to use the potatoes in the recipe, drain the water.

ITALIAN STROMBOLI

Serves 4 to 5

The beauty of stromboli is that you can fill it with your choice of fillings. This is a recipe that we all enjoy.

1. Preheat the oven to 350°F. Grease a 13 x 9-inch pan; set aside.

2. On a greased countertop, roll out the dough into a 15 x 10-inch rectangle. In a bowl, combine the canola oil with the parsley, oregano, and garlic powder. Brush this mixture over the dough. Sprinkle with 1½ cups of the shredded cheese. Add cooked sausage, mini pepperoni, diced ham, and hard salami. Sprinkle with the remaining 1½ cups shredded cheese.

3. Roll up the dough jelly roll style, starting with the long edge. Pinch seams and edges to seal it shut. Place the stromboli seam side down in the prepared pan. Brush the top with beaten egg whites. Do not allow the dough to rise. Bake at 350°F for 35 to 40 minutes, or until golden brown.

4. Cut into 10 slices and serve with warm pizza sauce, if desired.

1 pound frozen bread dough, thawed, or 1 pound Pizza Crust dough (p. 180)

1 tablespoon canola oil

1 teaspoon dried parsley

1 teaspoon dried oregano

½ teaspoon garlic powder

3 cups shredded mozzarella and provolone cheese blend, divided

1 pound ground country sausage, cooked and drained

5 ounces mini pepperoni

½ cup diced shaved ham

8 thin slices hard salami

2 egg whites, beaten

CHEESY BROWN SUGAR PORK CHOPS

Serves 6

Juicy and cheesy is the best way to describe these pork chops.

1 tablespoon minced fresh garlic

¼ cup packed brown sugar

6 boneless pork chops (about 3 pounds)

6 tablespoons (¾ stick) butter, cut into 6 even slices

1 teaspoon paprika

Garlic salt

Pepper

1 cup shredded Colby Jack cheese

1. Preheat the oven to 350°F. Stir together the minced garlic and brown sugar in a small bowl, then rub on both sides of the pork chops. Place the seasoned chops in a greased baking pan. Place 1 tablespoon butter on top of each pork chop. Sprinkle evenly with paprika and garlic salt and pepper as desired.

2. Bake, uncovered, at 350°F for 25 minutes. Remove the pork chops from the oven and sprinkle the shredded cheese over the chops. Turn the oven to a low broil and broil the pork chops for just a few minutes until the cheese is bubbled and lightly golden.

SWEETS

Dessert is always a perfect way to finish off a meal. I love to make desserts of all kinds. I always jokingly said that I should have had a house full of boys instead of girls to eat all the sweets I made!

FROSTED BANANA BARS

Yields 1 (17 x 12-inch) baking pan

My mom always made these when it was her turn to prepare church lunch, and I still remember how good these fluffy bars were with their generous layer of sweet frosting over top.

1. Preheat the oven to 325°F. In a large bowl, beat the butter and sugar together well. Add eggs, mashed bananas, half the flour, and vanilla. Mix well. In a 2-cup liquid measure, mix vinegar and milk and let stand for about 5 minutes. Stir into the batter, then add the remaining ingredients, mixing well.

2. Pour into a greased 17 x 12-inch baking pan and bake at 325°F for 30 to 40 minutes. Allow to cool partially, then frost with Brown Butter Frosting.

3. *To make Brown Butter Frosting:* Melt the butter and let it gently sizzle over medium heat, stirring often with a rubber spatula. When the butter puffs up and foams, it is ready to be removed from the heat. (This will take several minutes.) When the butter is browned, remove from heat and mix in powdered sugar and vanilla, then add enough milk to reach desired spreading consistency.

¾ cup (1½ sticks) butter, at room temperature

2¼ cups sugar

3 eggs

1½ cups mashed bananas

3 cups flour

1½ teaspoons vanilla extract

3 tablespoons vinegar

1 cup plus 2 tablespoons milk

1½ teaspoons baking soda

1½ teaspoons baking powder

¾ teaspoon salt

Brown Butter Frosting

1 cup (2 sticks) butter, browned gently on the stove until delicate brown

4 cups powdered sugar

2 teaspoons vanilla extract

About 6 tablespoons milk

FROSTED SUGAR COOKIE BARS

Yields 1 (18 x 13-inch) half-sheet baking pan

If you love frosted sugar cookies but need something a bit quicker and easier, these sugar cookie bars are a close match. They don't last long in our house!

1½ cups (3 sticks) butter, at room temperature

3 eggs

4 cups plus 1 tablespoon flour

2¼ cups sugar

1 tablespoon baking powder

¾ teaspoon salt

¾ teaspoon vanilla extract

¾ teaspoon almond extract

Buttercream Frosting

1 cup (2 sticks) butter, at room temperature

1 cup vegetable shortening (I prefer Crisco brand)

¼ teaspoon salt

1 teaspoon vanilla extract

1 teaspoon almond extract

8 cups powdered sugar

About 6 tablespoons milk

Sprinkles, for sprinkling (optional)

1. Preheat the oven to 350°F. Mix all the bar ingredients together. Press dough into a lightly greased 18 x 13-inch half-sheet baking pan. Bake at 350°F for 20 to 25 minutes, or until just lightly golden. Cool completely, then frost with Buttercream Frosting. Add sprinkles if desired.

2. *To make Buttercream Frosting:* Beat the butter and shortening together until light and fluffy. Beat in salt, vanilla, and almond extract. Slowly add powdered sugar and milk to the desired spreading consistency.

CRISPY RICE CARAMEL BARS

Yields 1 (13 x 9-inch) pan

This recipe is another one of Grandma Hartter's classic bars. It takes the ordinary Rice Krispie treat to the next level. It's a delight to take a bite of these gooey yet crunchy bars.

1. In a large microwavable bowl, melt ¼ cup (½ stick) of the butter and 4 cups of the marshmallows together until smooth. Add 4 cups of the cereal and mix well. Press this mixture into a greased 13 x 9-inch pan. (*Tip:* It works well to butter your hands to press the mixture into the pan. Note, too, that this full step is repeated later in the process.)

2. In a small pot on the stove, melt the caramels, ½ cup plus 2 tablespoons (1¼ sticks) of the butter, and sweetened condensed milk together over low to medium heat. Slowly increase the heat, stirring continuously with a flat wooden or rubber spatula so that it does not scorch. Let it bubble for 30 to 40 seconds, then immediately remove it from the heat. Pour this hot caramel mixture over the layer of cereal in the pan and spread evenly over all. Refrigerate, uncovered, for 1½ hours.

3. Repeat the first cereal layer over top, melting the remaining ¼ cup (½ stick) butter and 4 cups marshmallows together until completely smooth, then adding 4 cups cereal and mixing well. Press the cereal smoothly into the refrigerated caramel layer in the pan.

4. Store in a cool place. These are easy to nibble on!

1 cup plus 2 tablespoons (2¼ sticks) butter, divided

8 cups miniature marshmallows, divided

8 cups crisp rice cereal, divided

1 (11-ounce) bag baking caramels (I prefer Kraft brand), unwrapped

1 (13-ounce) can sweetened condensed milk

SCOTCHEROO BARS

Yields 1 (13 x 9-inch) pan

Another bar that always wins the popularity vote! Its chewy texture is packed with peanut butter flavor and topped with a layer of creamy chocolate mixture.

1 cup sugar

1¼ cups light corn syrup

1 cup creamy peanut butter

½ teaspoon vanilla extract

Dash salt

6 cups crisp rice cereal

1 (11-ounce) bag milk chocolate and peanut butter baking chips (I prefer Nestle brand)

1. In a medium-size pot on the stove, whisk the sugar and light corn syrup together, heating over low-medium heat just until it starts to bubble around the edges. It is important to remove it from the heat as soon as it starts to lightly bubble.

2. As soon as you remove the pot from the heat, mix in the peanut butter, vanilla, and salt. Stir well until the peanut butter is melted and the mixture is smooth. Add the cereal, stirring well with a large spoon. Using buttered hands, press this mixture into a greased 13 x 9-inch pan.

3. Put the chocolate and peanut butter chips into a small microwavable bowl. Microwave for about 5 minutes at power level 4, stirring often, just until it is melted and smooth. Do not heat too fast or too hot, or the chocolate will "seize," meaning it will clump up and not melt. You cannot reverse chocolate if it gets to this state.

4. Spread the melted mixture evenly over the bars. Let it stand at room temperature, uncovered, for 3 to 4 hours to let it naturally firm up. Do not refrigerate. Store bars at room temperature in a sealed container. The prepared bars can be frozen; just pull them out to thaw a couple of hours before serving.

MONSTER BARS

Yields 1 (18 x 13-inch) half-sheet baking pan

If you need a good classic bar for your next potluck or group gathering, this one is it.

1. Preheat the oven to 350°F. Beat the butter, granulated sugar, and brown sugar together in a large bowl. Add the eggs, vanilla, corn syrup, and baking soda. Mix well for 2 to 3 minutes, or until the mixture feels light and fluffy.

2. Stir in the creamy peanut butter until all mixed in. Gently stir in the oats, just until combined. Do not overmix. Stir in the milk chocolate chips.

3. Grease an 18 x 13-inch half-sheet baking pan and lightly press the dough into the pan. (It works well to wet the bottom of a measuring cup to press the dough.) Sprinkle the mini candy-coated chocolate pieces on top and lightly press into the dough.

4. Bake at 350°F for 12 minutes. (*Note:* The bars will not look done, but they will finish cooking as they sit.) Allow to cool for at least 1 hour before cutting into bars.

½ cup (1 stick) butter, at room temperature

1 cup granulated sugar

1 cup packed brown sugar

3 eggs

2 teaspoons vanilla extract

1 teaspoon light corn syrup

2 teaspoons baking soda

1½ cups creamy peanut butter

4½ cups quick-cooking oats

1 cup milk chocolate chips

1 cup mini candy-coated chocolate pieces

HEIDI'S SO-EASY SUGAR COOKIES

Yields 1 (18 x 13-inch) half-sheet baking pan

This recipe is from my sister-in-law Heidi. This is the easiest version of sugar cookies I have encountered. They literally melt in your mouth. The best part of these cookies is all the little baked scraps in between the cutouts . . . What do you do with scraps? You eat them! I finally realized I could also cut them in bars to utilize the whole pan, but there is something special about nibbling on those tiny pieces. See what you think!

1½ cups sugar

½ cup plus 2⅔ tablespoons (1⅓ sticks) butter, at room temperature

⅔ cup canola oil

2 eggs

2 tablespoons milk

1 tablespoon almond extract

3 cups flour

1 tablespoon baking powder

½ teaspoon salt

Colored sugar (optional)

1. Preheat the oven to 375°F. Using a hand mixer, beat the sugar, butter, oil, eggs, milk, and almond extract together until light and fluffy. Add the flour, baking powder, and salt, mixing well. Spread into a greased 18 x 13-inch half-sheet baking pan. I use a small, angled spreader to make it as smooth as possible.

2. Sprinkle with colored sugar, if desired. This is fun to vary with the seasons.

3. Bake at 375°F for 10 to 12 minutes—no longer. Remove from the oven and let cool for 5 minutes. After 5 minutes, cut into shapes with a cookie cutter, or cut into bars.

4. Let the pan cool completely; then, using a small cookie spatula, remove the cutout cookies to serve. The remaining scraps are yours to nibble on!

MOM'S MILK CHOCOLATE CHIP COOKIES

Yields 4 dozen cookies

My mom is known for her Milk Chocolate Chip Cookies! Even today, it is a rare day if Mom doesn't have a container of these stuffed away in the freezer for weekend guests, potlucks, family gatherings, and once in a while "just because." Although we all follow Mom's recipe to a T . . . we agree that they still don't taste quite like hers. But this version—a Homestead favorite—is still perfect every time.

Mom always taught me that the key to delicious cookies is to not overbake them. As young girls, we eagerly watched them in the oven and waited until they just barely started turning a pale light golden brown around the edges. This meant that they were ready to come out of the oven! We had to wait a few more minutes to let them cool down enough to eat those warm, fresh cookies. By the time we were cleaning the kitchen, we were stuffed with cookie dough and warm cookies. Even today, Mom still likes to treat us to her cookies when we visit, and we still love it.

1. Preheat the oven to 350°F. Using a mixer, beat the shortening, brown sugar, granulated sugar, and vanilla together on high speed until light and fluffy, 3 to 4 minutes. Add the eggs and continue to beat well.

2. Mix in the salt, baking soda, and flour until well mixed. Add milk chocolate chips and stir in until evenly incorporated.

3. Shape the dough into 1-inch balls, rolling in the palm of your hand until smooth. Place the balls on a lightly greased baking sheet. Do not flatten these cookies. Bake at 350°F for 7 to 8 minutes. Watch closely and remove from the oven as soon as you start seeing a light golden edge and shallow cracks on top of the cookies. It is important to remember not to overbake cookies.

2 cups vegetable shortening (I prefer Crisco brand)

2 cups packed brown sugar

1 cup granulated sugar

2 teaspoons vanilla extract

4 eggs

2 teaspoons salt

2 slightly rounded teaspoons baking soda

4 cups flour

1 (11.5-ounce) bag milk chocolate chips

Pepper nuts

1 cup lard (or 2 cups oleo
1 cup butter)
1 cup sour cream
1/2 teas. lemon oil
2 cups brown sugar
1 cup white sugar
1 egg
1 teas. each: allspice, cinnamon,
nutmeg, ginger, soda, baking powder,
and black pepper.

1/4 teas. salt
1 cup flour
    Cream shortening and sugar together.
Add egg and lemon oil. Sift flour,
flour, soda, baking powder and salt
together. Add alternately with sour cream.
Remove from mixer and stir in 4 1/2 cups
flour, then cut long rolls the size of a
finger and length of cookie sheet. Reduce
the chill and freeze. Slice and bake at
375 until light brown, approximately 10-15 min.
store in tight containers.

-23-

GRANDMA HARTTER'S CHRISTMAS PEPPERNUTS

Yields 2 (1-gallon) ice cream buckets

Oh, the sweet memories I have of being at Grandpa and Grandma Hartter's house. I remember their big house in the country, with its open staircase, Ben Franklin woodstove, deep green shag carpet, creaking upstairs floors, Aunt Judy and Aunt Teresa's hot pink room with the Swiss Chalet music box, Grandma's candy drawer . . . the list could go on and on! Most of all, I remember Christmas—the skits, the rows of stockings that lined the open staircase, Grandpa's nut bowl with the nutcracker, the real Christmas tree, and most of all the warmth, love, and laughter of family.

Every Christmas, we could count on Grandma's figure-eight Norwegian Kringla and crunchy peppernuts. I especially loved it when she pulled out the ice cream buckets of peppernuts. We ate these tiny, crunchy little spice cookies by the handful. For me, this cookie is about the memories we made during those Christmases together. We were blessed with such a legacy of love, and I hope that I never take that for granted. Some sweet day, I look forward to meeting again.

1. Using a stand mixer or a hand mixer, beat together the shortening, butter, and brown sugar. Add the egg and anise oil. In a separate bowl, combine the spices, pepper, baking soda, baking powder, salt, and 1 cup of the flour, then add this mixture to the shortening mixture alternately with the sour cream. Beat together. Continue to gradually add the remaining 6½ cups flour while mixing on low speed.

2. Roll pieces of dough into long rolls, the width of a finger and the length of a baking sheet. Repeat until finished. Freeze on baking sheets for 4 hours (it helps if they are not touching). Slice into small ½-inch coins and place on greased baking sheets about ¼ inch apart.

3. Preheat the oven to 375°F. Bake at 375°F for 8 to 10 minutes, or until lightly browned and crispy. Allow to cook, then freeze in ice cream buckets or other large containers. I recommend eating them by the handful!

1 cup vegetable shortening (I prefer Crisco brand)

1 cup (2 sticks) butter, at room temperature

2 cups packed brown sugar

1 egg

½ teaspoon anise oil

1 teaspoon ground allspice

1 teaspoon ground cinnamon

1 teaspoon ground nutmeg

1 teaspoon ground ginger

1 teaspoon pepper

1 teaspoon baking soda

1 teaspoon baking powder

½ teaspoon salt

7½ cups flour, divided

1 cup sour cream

pleasant
words are as
an honeycomb,
sweet to the soul,
and health to
the bones.

PROVERBS 16:24

SPRITZ CHRISTMAS COOKIES

Yields 15 dozen cookies

Whenever my mom got out her old vintage metal cookie press, we kids would be so excited—it was time for these Spritz Christmas Cookies! We had so much fun watching her put the plate in and press out the little green trees and white poinsettia flowers. She always colored part of the dough green to press the trees and left part of it uncolored for the poinsettia flowers. Then she sprinkled the trees with colored nonpareils and placed a Red Hot cinnamon candy at the top and another into the center of the flowers. It is hard to eat just one of these cookies.

2 cups (4 sticks) butter, at room temperature

1½ cups sugar

2 eggs

1 teaspoon almond extract

5 cups flour

1 teaspoon baking powder

½ teaspoon salt

1. Preheat the oven to 400°F.

2. Beat the butter and sugar together until light and fluffy, about 5 minutes. Beat in the eggs and almond extract. In a separate bowl, stir together the flour, baking powder, and salt. Gradually add the flour mixture to the butter mixture. Mix until smooth.

3. Divide the dough in half. Color one half green and leave the other half as is. Using a cookie press and the plate of your choice, press the little cookies out onto a lightly greased baking sheet. (It will work best if you press out the uncolored dough first.) Bake at 400°F for 7 to 8 minutes, or until the cookies are just barely light golden around the edges. Do not overbake.

4. Decorate as desired. Allow to cool completely, then carefully loosen them from the tray using a small cookie spatula. Freeze.

NO-BAKE COOKIES

Yields 3 dozen cookies

Warning! These cookies are hard to resist.

1. On the stovetop, bring the sugar, milk, cocoa powder, and butter to a boil. Continue to boil for 1 minute. Remove the saucepan from the heat and stir in the remaining ingredients until well blended.

2. Shape into balls and flatten them on a parchment-lined baking sheet. Freeze and package.

2 cups sugar

1 cup milk

⅔ cup unsweetened cocoa powder

½ cup (1 stick) butter

1 cup creamy peanut butter

2 tablespoons vanilla extract

4 cups quick-cooking oats

2 cups crisp rice cereal

Tip: These cookies are easier to handle when they are frozen. They can be packaged into small containers for the freezer and enjoyed when you need a quick chocolate treat. They thaw quickly.

APPLE CRISP

Serves 5 to 6

Enjoy this classic crisp with a mound of vanilla ice cream and drizzled with caramel sauce.

6 Gala or Pink Lady apples, peeled and chopped

2 tablespoons granulated sugar

1¾ teaspoons ground cinnamon, divided

1½ teaspoons lemon juice

1 cup packed brown sugar

¾ cup flour

¾ cup old-fashioned oats

½ cup (1 stick) butter, at room temperature

Pinch salt

1. Preheat the oven to 350°F. Grease an 8 x 8-inch baking dish. In a mixing bowl, combine the chopped apples, sugar, 1 teaspoon of the cinnamon, and lemon juice. Pour this mixture into the greased pan.

2. In a separate bowl, combine the remaining ¾ teaspoon cinnamon, brown sugar, flour, oats, butter, and salt. Mix with a fork or pastry cutter until crumbly. Spread this mixture over the apples. Sprinkle with a little more cinnamon.

3. Bake at 350°F for about 45 minutes, or until golden and bubbly.

4. Let the crisp stand for 15 minutes, then serve warm with vanilla ice cream and caramel sauce, if desired.

FLAKY PIE CRUST

Yields 4 to 5 (9-inch) pie crusts

A nice flaky homemade pie crust is what really sets a pie apart. I usually use Crisco vegetable shortening, but you may also substitute lard, if desired.

1. Using a pastry cutter, blend the flour, shortening, and salt until it has the consistency of fine crumbs. In a separate bowl, whisk together the vinegar, egg, cold water, and sugar. Add this to the crumb mixture. Toss it all together with a fork until just mixed. Cover with plastic wrap and refrigerate for 15 minutes.

2. Depending on the size of your pie pans, divide the dough into four or five balls. Roll crusts and fill each pie pan. (If you plan to freeze crusts for longer-term storage, you may wish to use aluminum pie pans.) Using a paring knife, cut excess pie crust from around the edge to create a clean edge. Flute the crust edge, if desired. (Don't forget to sprinkle any scraps with cinnamon and sugar and bake them for a few minutes at 350°F for a sweet treat!)

3. To freeze prepared pie crusts, place a sheet of plastic wrap over each pan to keep the frozen crusts separated. Stack the pans up to five crusts high. Wrap the entire stack tightly with plastic wrap, label, date, and freeze for future pie-baking days. To use a frozen pie crust, remove it from the freezer. Unwrap it and let it thaw at room temperature for 30 to 60 minutes, then proceed to make your pie.

4 cups all-purpose flour (pastry flour also works)

1¾ cups vegetable shortening

2 teaspoons salt

1 tablespoon white vinegar

1 egg

½ cup ice cold water

¼ teaspoon sugar

PREBAKED PIE SHELL

When a recipe calls for a prebaked pie shell, poke the crust generously with a fork on the bottom and around the sides of the pan. Preheat the oven to 350°F. Grease a lightweight aluminum foil pie pan and lightly set it over top the crust. Keeping the pans together, gently flip them upside down. Bake, upside-down, at 350°F for 7 minutes. (Do not turn off the oven.) Flip the pie crust and pans right side up and remove the top foil pan. Continue to bake the pie crust for another 10 to 15 minutes, or until it is light golden and just barely starts cracking in the middle. Cool, then fill as directed.

PREPARING PIE CRUSTS

Mom always made rolling look easy as she rolled the dough between sheets of lightly floured wax paper, carefully flipping, peeling back the wax paper to adjust, and rolling again until it was just the right thickness. I loved to watch her gently lay the dough in the pan, peel back the wax paper, effortlessly and smoothly cut off the excess dough at the rim of the pan, and then work her magic by fluting the crust.

She liked to keep these pie crusts wrapped tightly in the freezer for pie baking days. It was such a treat when there were a few scraps left over; she would roll the pie crust scraps out onto small sheets of aluminum foil, brush them with butter and then sugar and cinnamon, and pop them in the oven for us. We watched as they puffed slightly and started to sizzle around the edge, creating a nice light golden crust. We couldn't eat them too soon, or we would burn our tongues. There was never enough to share, in our opinion, but that's what made these pie dough patches so special. I did the same for my own girls on my pie baking days, and I hope they treasure the same memory.

PIE FRIES WITH CHERRY PIE FILLING

Serves 10 to 12

Back in the early days of The Homestead (when I must have had more time!), I enjoyed creating these pie fries for customers. We stuffed them in small French fry pockets and served them with a small cup of pie filling for dipping. They were fun and made a good conversation piece. If you love pie crust, you will likely love these pie fries. Experiment with different flavors if you'd like—you could even dip them in icing.

1. If using a frozen, premade batch of Flaky Pie Crust, take it out of the freezer to thaw. Preheat the oven to 350°F. Roll balls of dough as you would a pie crust, only thicker. I try to roll it ¼ to ⅜ inch thick. Brush the dough with melted butter and sprinkle with coarse sugar and cinnamon.

2. Using a pizza cutter, cut strips of cinnamon-sugar pie dough ⅝ to ¾ inches wide and 3½ to 4 inches long. Gently lift the strips onto a parchment-lined baking sheet. Bake at 350°F for 10 to 15 minutes, or until the "fries" are light golden. Remove from the oven and allow to cool completely. If you have extra fries, these will freeze nicely to serve later.

3. *To make Cherry Pie Filling:* Stir together the cherries, sugar, cold water, cornstarch, and lemon juice on the stove and heat until thickened. Remove from heat and stir in the almond extract. This filling is delicious served warm with pie fries.

1 batch Flaky Pie Crust (p. 272)

½ cup (1 stick) butter, melted

Coarse sugar

Ground cinnamon

Cherry Pie Filling

3 cups sour pie cherries, pitted

1 cup sugar

¼ cup cold water

¼ cup cornstarch or Thermflo

½ teaspoon lemon juice

1½ teaspoons almond extract

BLUEBERRY CREAM PIE

Yields 1 (9-inch) pie

My dad always says he likes two kinds of pie . . . hot and cold! We loved to come home from school and find a pot of chili and a freshly baked pie sitting on the counter for supper that evening. Mom made a lot of cream pies using a variety of fruits, depending on what was in season. Her apple cream pie used the tart summer apples, and peach cream was best when ripe, juicy peaches were in season. Now that I live in Indiana, we have access to abundant fresh blueberries, so we enjoy this pie with blueberries and cream.

1¼ cups sugar

1 cup half-and-half

½ cup flour or Thermflo

1 teaspoon vanilla extract

Dash salt

3½ cups fresh blueberries

1 (9-inch) unbaked pie shell (see Flaky Pie Crust, p. 272)

Crumble topping

2 tablespoons (¼ stick) butter, melted

¼ cup sugar

¼ cup flour

Ground cinnamon

1. Preheat the oven to 350°F. Whisk the sugar, half-and-half, flour, vanilla, and salt together. (I like to microwave this mixture for 1 to 2 minutes to warm it up.) Carefully stir in the fresh blueberries.

2. Fill the unbaked pie shell with the blueberry cream mixture. Be careful not to overfill, or the pie may run over when baking. (*Tip:* I like to bake my pies on a parchment-lined baking sheet pan to catch any drips that ooze over the pie. It saves a lot of clean-up later.)

3. *To make crumble topping:* In a small bowl, mix together the melted butter, sugar, and flour. Evenly sprinkle this over the top of the pie. Lightly sprinkle with cinnamon.

4. Bake at 350°F for 1 hour, or until pie puffs up and bubbles in the middle and the topping is light golden. Cool for at least 1 hour before cutting. It is delicious served warm!

SUGAR CREAM PIE

Serves 6 to 8

When I married Mike and moved to Indiana, I had never heard of sugar cream pie. I was quickly introduced to the Indiana state pie, and it is now one of my favorites. Even my Kansas family enjoys this one. This Sugar Cream Pie is also one of our top-selling pies at The Homestead. Its rich, creamy filling is smooth and sweet, with just the right amount of cinnamon sprinkled on top. It is delicious either warm or cold.

1. Preheat the oven to 350°F.

2. Whisk the milk, sugar, and cornstarch together over medium heat, stirring continuously so it does not scorch. Cook it until it thickens, then remove from heat. Add the butter and vanilla and continue to stir until it is melted and smooth. Pour into the pre-baked pie shell. Sprinkle the top with ground cinnamon.

3. Bake at 350°F for 5 minutes. Remove from the oven and allow to cool.

2⅔ cups milk

1⅓ cup sugar

¼ cup plus 3 tablespoons cornstarch or Thermflo

½ cup (1 stick) plus 2½ tablespoons butter, at room temperature

1½ teaspoons vanilla extract

1 (9-inch) prebaked pie shell (see Flaky Pie Crust, p. 272)

Ground cinnamon

MILE-HIGH MERINGUE

Yields enough meringue for 1 (9-inch) pie

Making meringue always intimidated me, but I love a good meringue on a pie. This meringue never fails, and your pie will look professionally made with its light golden sweet mount on top. This meringue works for prepared pies that use a prebaked crust. It is made with just two ingredients—couldn't be easier!

4 egg whites

1 (7-ounce) jar marshmallow cream

1 (9-inch) prepared cream pie of your choice (such as coconut, banana, chocolate, butterscotch)

1. Preheat the oven to 350°F. Using a high-powered mixer with a wire whisk, beat the egg whites on high for 7 to 9 minutes until they stand in stiff peaks.

2. Mix in the marshmallow cream and continue to beat for an additional 2 to 3 minutes until the meringue is thick and glossy.

3. Immediately spread the meringue over the filling in the prepared cream pie. Using a small, angled spreader, spread the meringue completely to the edges of the prebaked pie shell and fluff and arrange the meringue over the pie to create a beautiful mound.

4. Bake at 350°F for 10 to 12 minutes, or until the meringue is nice and golden. Watch closely so it doesn't get too dark.

5. Remove the pie from the oven and let it cool before slicing. Keep refrigerated.

PUMPKIN PIE DESSERT

Serves 12 to 15

We love traditional pumpkin pie—in fact, it's Mike's favorite pie. This 13 x 9-inch pan dessert is a glorified pumpkin pie and is easy to serve to a crowd. Serve chilled with a hefty dollop of sweetened whipped cream.

1. Preheat the oven to 350°F. Combine the ½ cup melted butter, flour, oats, and brown sugar in a small bowl. Mix until crumbly and press into a greased 13 x 9-inch pan.

2. In a separate large bowl, beat together the pumpkin, evaporated milk, eggs, sugar, spices, and salt. Pour this mixture into the crust.

3. Bake at 350°F for 45 to 60 minutes, or until the center is not quite set (it should still jiggle slightly when you shake it gently). While it bakes, combine the topping ingredients until crumbly. Sprinkle the topping over the top of the partially baked pumpkin mixture, then continue baking at 350°F for an *additional* 15 to 20 minutes, or until the center is set. Allow to cool, then refrigerate.

½ cup (1 stick) butter, melted

1 cup flour

½ cup quick-cooking oats

½ cup packed brown sugar

2 (15-ounce) cans pumpkin puree

2 (12-ounce) cans evaporated milk

4 eggs

1½ cups sugar

2 teaspoons ground cinnamon

1 teaspoon ground ginger

½ teaspoon ground cloves

1 teaspoon salt

Topping

2 tablespoons butter, melted

½ cup packed brown sugar

½ cup chopped pecans

PUMPKIN WHIP

Serves 8 to 10

We enjoy this super easy whipped dessert in the fall. It is light and so refreshing, especially if you are one of those people who love all things pumpkin. Fill individual dessert cups that are almost too pretty to eat, or pair it with some chewy Gingersnap Cookies (p. 287) as a garnish or for a wonderful trifle dessert (see sidebar).

1 (15-ounce) can pumpkin puree (not pumpkin pie mix)

3 cups milk

1½ teaspoons ground cinnamon

2 (3.4-ounce) boxes instant butterscotch pudding

8 ounces frozen nondairy whipped topping

1. With a wire whisk or electric mixer on low, whip the pumpkin, milk, cinnamon, and instant pudding mix until smooth and well combined. Refrigerate until firm. Gently stir/whip in whipped topping until smooth.

2. Enjoy the whip served in a bowl.

- Try pairing Pumpkin Whip with Gingersnap Cookies (p. 287) for some delicious variations:
- Serve in individual 9-ounce clear cups with a dollop of extra whipped topping and a sprinkle of cinnamon on top. Stick a small, soft gingersnap cookie in the whipped topping as a fun garnish. This makes for a very pretty display!
- Make individual 9-ounce trifle cups, building with layers of Pumpkin Whip, small cubes of Gingersnap Cookies, more Pumpkin Whip, and frozen nondairy whipped topping. Sprinkle ground cinnamon over the whipped topping and garnish with half a Gingersnap Cookie.
- Make a large trifle bowl that guests dip out with a spoon—an easy dessert for a large group. Follow the same outline above, just in a larger serving bowl. There's no right or wrong way to do this . . . just make it look pretty!

GINGERSNAP COOKIES

Yields 3 dozen cookies

The secret to a delightful gingersnap is to not overbake it. You will agree when you take a bite of this chewy cookie bursting with flavorful spice.

1. Preheat the oven to 350°F.

2. Beat the shortening and sugar together until light and fluffy, about 5 minutes. Add eggs and molasses and beat well again.

3. In a separate bowl, combine the flour, baking soda, cinnamon, ginger, cloves, and salt. Add to the egg mixture. Shape into small balls and roll in sugar.

4. Bake at 350°F for 7 to 8 minutes, or just until done. Be careful not to overbake. These are better if they are a little chewy.

1½ cups butter-flavored vegetable shortening

2 cups sugar plus more for rolling

2 eggs

½ cup molasses

4 cups flour

2 teaspoons baking soda

2 teaspoons ground cinnamon

2 teaspoons ground ginger

1 teaspoon ground cloves

¼ teaspoon salt

DESSERT PIZZA BREADSTICKS

Yields 2 (16-inch) pizza pans

These soft, sweet breadsticks are a perfect finale to any meal. The recipe can be halved to make just one pan, if desired.

1 batch Pizza Crust dough (p. 180)

¼ cup (½ stick) butter, melted, plus additional for brushing after baking

⅓ cup granulated sugar

2 teaspoons ground cinnamon

Icing

2 cups powdered sugar

½ teaspoon vanilla extract

½ teaspoon almond extract

3 to 4 tablespoons milk

1. Preheat the oven to 425°F. If you haven't done so already, divide the pizza dough into two even sections. Roll the dough directly onto a large, greased, seasoned pizza stone, preferably a flat stone with no lip (or use a pizza pan or other pan). Roll the crust completely to the stone's rim. Using a pastry brush, brush ¼ cup melted butter over the dough.

2. Combine the sugar and cinnamon and sprinkle the mixture over the dough, covering completely. Using a pizza cutter, cut the dough in half across the length of the stone. Then cut perpendicularly in 1- to 1¼-inch-wide slices. (For smaller serving sizes, first cut in thirds, then perpendicularly.) Set the stone aside to proof the dough for 15 to 20 minutes.

3. Bake at 425°F for about 15 minutes, or until the breadsticks are puffy and lightly golden. Remove from the oven and brush with additional melted butter. Let cool for 15 minutes.

4. *To make icing:* Mix all the icing ingredients together, starting with 3 tablespoons milk and adding more to desired consistency.

5. Drizzle breadsticks with icing. Serve warm.

RUSTIC CHERRY GALETTE

Serves 6 to 8

Here in the Midwest, we love our pie! Galettes aren't as popular, but they are just as delicious. I love the rugged, flaky crust filled with pie filling. These are also very easy to make and are a fast alternative when you want the pie flavor without all the work.

1. *To make Cherry Pie Filling:* Combine all the filling ingredients in a medium pot. Heat the mixture on the stove until it thickens, stirring constantly. Remove from heat and allow to cool down.

2. *To make crust:* In the meantime, using a pastry cutter, mix the cold butter and shortening with the flour, sugar, and salt. Drizzle with the water. Remove the dough from the bowl and pat into a round disk. Wrap the dough disk in plastic wrap and refrigerate for 45 minutes.

3. Preheat the oven to 350°F.

4. After the dough has chilled for 45 minutes, roll it out into a 12-inch diameter circle on a lightly floured flat baking stone or baking sheet. Mend any cracks or tears by pressing them together. Using an upside-down 9-inch pie pan, lightly press it into the center of the dough to make a slight indentation. This is your filling indicator line. Fill the circle with the cooled filling. Fold the rim of dough up and over the edge of the filling, overlapping and pleating as you go. Brush the crust with heavy cream and sprinkle with coarse sugar.

5. Bake at 350°F for 35 to 45 minutes, or until the crust becomes lightly golden. Cool and slice. Enjoy with a bowl of ice cream!

Cherry Pie Filling

2 cups sour pie cherries, pitted

¼ cup granulated sugar

¼ cup packed brown sugar

4 teaspoons cornstarch or Thermflo

½ teaspoon almond extract

Dash salt

2 drops red food color (optional)

Crust

6 tablespoons cold butter

2 tablespoons vegetable shortening

1½ cups flour

1 tablespoon sugar

⅛ teaspoon salt

¼ cup ice cold water

Heavy cream, for brushing

Coarse sugar, for sprinkling

WHITE CHOCOLATE CHEESECAKE

Serves 12 to 14

Our daughter Kenzie took an interest in learning to bake cheesecake, and this is one that she mastered. We've served it several times for special occasions. It is so creamy and smooth. Add toppings as desired.

Crust

5 tablespoons butter

4 ounces white chocolate, chopped

1½ cups graham cracker crumbs

Filling

4½ (4-ounce) bars white chocolate

¼ cup heavy cream

3 (8-ounce) packages cream cheese, at room temperature

½ cup sugar

½ cup sour cream

4 eggs

1 tablespoon vanilla extract

White Chocolate Glaze

½ cup heavy cream

1 tablespoon butter

2 (4-ounce) bars white chocolate

1. *To make crust*: Melt the butter and white chocolate, then mix in graham cracker crumbs. Press mixture into a 9-inch springform pan. Refrigerate. When the crust is completely chilled, place the springform pan inside a slightly larger cake pan and set aside. Preheat the oven to 275°F.

2. *To make filling:* In another saucepan, melt the white chocolate bars and heavy cream together, then remove from heat to cool slightly. Set aside. In a large mixing bowl, beat together the cream cheese and sugar. Add sour cream, eggs, and vanilla. Beat in the cooled white chocolate mixture. Pour the filling atop the crust inside the springform pan. Place the springform pan/cake pan combo into an even larger rectangular pan (like a deep aluminum foil pan) and fill this pan halfway with water. This will prevent the cheesecake from cracking while it bakes and cools.

3. Bake at 275°F for 1 hour, then turn the oven down to 250°F and bake for an additional 1 hour. After baking is finished, turn the oven off *but do not open the door.* Leave the cheesecake in the oven (with the door closed) for 1 hour. Carefully remove the springform pan from the oven (you can discard the water in the large pan). Refrigerate cheesecake for 8 hours or overnight.

4. *To make White Chocolate Glaze:* Add the heavy cream and butter to a small pan and bring to a simmer. Put the white chocolate in a separate bowl and pour the warmed mixture over it, stirring until incorporated. Allow the glaze to cool, then spoon or pour it over the cold, refrigerated cheesecake. Enjoy!

VANILLA PUDDING

Serves 4 to 6

I remember our first home microwave, a brand-new Amana Radarange—sometime in the early 1980s. That amazing oven could heat things in just a few minutes. It could even cook! Times were advancing, and it was a dream to not have to melt butter on the stovetop any longer. Included with the new microwave was a cookbook of recipes to try. Mom tested the Vanilla Pudding recipe using the new microwave, and we loved it!

This pudding was one of the first recipes I learned to make, along with tuna casserole, apple salad, and baked beans. We enjoyed it on many evenings at our family table. Often, Mom stretched it by putting slices of banana in the warm pudding. Other times, it was used as filling for a coconut cream pie. If using it for coconut cream pie filling, add 1½ cups sweetened shredded coconut with the butter and vanilla. This pudding is as comforting as a warm, fluffy blanket on a cold winter night.

1. Beat the egg yolks in a large bowl and set aside. In a microwavable bowl, heat the milk for 6 minutes on power level 8 and set aside. In a separate bowl, mix together the sugar, cornstarch, and salt, then slowly whisk in the hot milk. Slowly drizzle this mixture into the beaten egg yolks, whisking at the same time.

2. Cook the pudding mixture in the microwave on power level 8 until thickened. Stop and whisk it every couple of minutes until thickened. Stir in the vanilla and butter until melted. Cover with plastic wrap and let it cool to lukewarm to eat.

3 egg yolks

3 cups milk

¾ cup sugar

5 tablespoons cornstarch

½ teaspoon salt

2 teaspoons vanilla extract

2 tablespoons butter

WINTER NIGHT TAPIOCA

Serves 4 to 6

This is probably the humblest recipe of all. It's nothing fancy, nor does it claim elegance of any nature. Yet it is one of our fa- vorite recipes to enjoy on a cold winter night. It was one that the girls begged for, and even now that they are grown and enjoy families of their own, they still ask me to make it for them occasionally.

This recipe has been around awhile—I remember a time as a young girl when I got the notion to make it for supper. I had recently had tapioca at Grandma Hartter's, and she colored it pink. That color made an impression on me, so I thought I would try the same. And since I loved it so much, I decided I would double the batch. Well, my pink tapioca didn't turn out so well, and as I recall, all of it was tossed in the garbage! This is just one of my early stories in the kitchen—I've learned a few things along the way. But this tapioca recipe has been a constant comfort over all those years.

⅓ cup sugar

3 tablespoons minute tapioca

1 egg, beaten

2¾ cups milk

1 tablespoon vanilla extract

1. Combine the sugar, tapioca, beaten egg, and milk in a large stockpot. (The mixture will rise to a high bubble while cooking, so you'll want a pot with high sides.) Let it stand for 5 minutes. Place the pot on a medium heat until the mixture comes to a full boil. Stir this continuously with a flat spatula.

2. When the mixture comes to a full boil, remove from heat and stir in the vanilla. Set the pudding aside to cool down and thicken for at least 20 minutes. It is absolutely the best when it is enjoyed warm. It will comfort you from the inside out.

Note: Despite my unsuccessful attempt to double the batch years and years ago, you *can* double it—with delicious results! When the tapioca boils, it rises to a high bubble in the pot, so it is important to use a large pot when making tapioca, especially a double batch.

CHOCOLATE BUTTERMILK CAKE

Yields 1 (18 x 13-inch) half-sheet baking pan

Chocolate Buttermilk Cake is a Bahler family favorite. Mike's mom introduced me to this recipe, and I've used it ever since. Mike's favorite way to eat this cake is to cut a big slice and microwave it for a few seconds so that the frosting just starts to melt. I agree, that is an amazing way to enjoy this cake.

1. Preheat the oven to 400°F. Mix together the flour, sugar, and salt. Set aside. On the stovetop, combine the water, butter, and cocoa powder and bring to a boil. When this boils, remove it from heat and set aside.

2. In a large mixing bowl, combine the eggs, buttermilk, baking soda, and vanilla. Add the flour mixture and cocoa mixture and beat until smooth. Spread the batter into a lightly greased 18 x 13-inch half-sheet baking pan.

3. Bake at 400°F for 20 to 25 minutes, or just until the cake springs back when lightly touched. Test with a wooden pick inserted in the center of the cake; when the cake is done, it should come out cleanly. Remove from the oven and let cool for about 30 minutes, then frost with Chocolate Frosting. It is important to frost the cake while it is a little warm.

4. *To make Chocolate Frosting:* Beat together all the ingredients. You can add more milk or powdered sugar until frosting reaches desired consistency and taste. Spread on the cake while it is still a little warm.

3 cups flour

3 cups sugar

¾ teaspoon salt

1½ cups water

1½ cups (3 sticks) butter

⅓ cups unsweetened cocoa powder

3 eggs

⅓ cup buttermilk*

1½ teaspoons baking soda

1½ teaspoons vanilla extract

Chocolate Frosting

6 tablespoons (¾ stick) butter, melted

About ½ cup milk

⅓ cup unsweetened cocoa powder

1½ teaspoons vanilla extract

About 5 cups powdered sugar

* If you do not have buttermilk, you can make a buttermilk substitute with milk and vinegar: Pour 1 teaspoon white vinegar into a small liquid measuring cup. Add milk to the ⅓-cup line. Stir gently, then let this mixture sit for 5 minutes as the milk "sours" and thickens.

blessed
are they which
do hunger and
thirst after
righteousness:
for they shall
be filled.

MATTHEW 5:6

COCONUT CAKE

Yields 1 (13 x 9-inch) pan

I enjoy a light cake, and this coconut version of a poke cake is so refreshing. I love to serve it in the springtime, around Easter.

1 (15.25-ounce) box white cake mix

1½ teaspoons coconut extract

1 (15-ounce) can cream of coconut, shaken well

8 ounces frozen nondairy whipped topping

¼ cup instant vanilla pudding mix

1 teaspoon coconut extract

Toasted coconut flakes* (optional)

1. Preheat the oven and prepare the cake mix as directed on the box—*except omit any vanilla* and add 1½ teaspoons coconut extract instead. Bake as directed in a greased 13 x 9-inch cake pan.

2. Remove the cake from the oven and poke holes evenly and copiously over the entire cake with a fork. Pour the well-shaken can of coconut milk evenly over the top of the cake. Refrigerate, uncovered, for at least 2 hours.

3. Once the cake has completely chilled, it can be frosted. In a medium mixing bowl, beat together the whipped topping, instant vanilla pudding mix, and coconut extract. Spread over the cake. If desired, sprinkle the top of the cake with toasted coconut flakes.

4. Keep the cake refrigerated. This is so refreshing!

* You can make toasted coconut flakes in a skillet on the stove or in the oven. The oven method is easy and quick: Preheat the oven to 325°F. Spread coconut evenly on a rimmed baking sheet (don't layer it too thick). Bake at 325°F for 5 to 10 minutes, stirring often, until lightly golden and fragrant.

GERMAN CHOCOLATE CAKE

Yields 1 (9-inch) layer cake

When Mike's birthday rolls around, I know he'll love either Chocolate Buttermilk Cake (p. 299) or this German Chocolate Cake with a hefty dose of homemade frosting. I cheat and use a boxed cake mix, but the frosting should never be compromised by using a container from the grocery store.

1. Preheat the oven and mix the cake as directed on the box. Evenly pour the batter into two greased 9-inch cake pans and level it out. (You may wish to line the pan with circles of parchment paper for easy removal—grease the parchment paper and lightly sprinkle with flour.) Bake as directed. When the cake is done, remove it from the oven and let it cool completely. Carefully remove the fully cooled layers from the pans.

2. Meanwhile, in a pot on the stovetop, combine the butter, evaporated milk, beaten egg yolks, and sugar. Bring this mixture to a low boil, stirring constantly. As soon as it boils, turn the heat down to maintain a low bubble. Set the timer for 9 minutes and continue to cook, stirring constantly.

3. After 9 minutes, remove from heat and stir in the vanilla, shredded coconut, and chopped pecans. Let this frosting partially cool, then spread 2 cups frosting evenly over one layer of the fully cooled cake. Top with the second cake layer and add additional frosting on top.

Note: I have enlarged the frosting recipe to accommodate Mike's preference, so you may not need all of it. Extra frosting will freeze well.

1 (15.25-ounce) box German chocolate cake mix

¾ cup (1½ sticks) butter

1½ cups evaporated milk, shaken well

4 egg yolks, beaten

1½ cups sugar

1½ teaspoons vanilla extract

½ cup sweetened shredded coconut

1½ cups chopped pecans

HOMEMADE ICE CREAM

My father-in-law, Lowell, was known far and wide for his love of homemade ice cream. He cranked out gallons and gallons of delicious vanilla ice cream no matter the time of year. For him, ice cream was always in season! He loved to share it around town so others could enjoy.

When Mike and I married in 1993 and moved onto the homeplace, Dad and Mom moved off the farm and into town. Their large lawn on the north edge of town provided a perfect view of our town's annual fireworks show. Every July 4, a large crowd of family and friends gathered at Dad and Mom's for fireworks and homemade ice cream. It was always fun to see the variety of buckets and flavors brought in as we lined up five to six freezers on the garage counter. It was even more fun to dip into each one. Of course we wanted to try them all! We enjoyed flavors such as coffee chip, butter pecan, strawberry, Indiana blueberry, chocolate and chocolate chip, cookie dough, and even raspberry sorbet.

Dad always stuck with his vanilla recipe, but it was special, and so was he! Dad has gone on to his heavenly reward, and we miss his presence on warm summer nights as we continue to carry on his legacy and enjoy his favorite homemade ice cream. Dad was charmingly known as "Lil Jake" as a youngster (after his father, Jake). So we enjoy cranking out Lil Jake's ice cream at The Homestead in his sweet memory. Mom continues to open her home and lawn to family and friends on the Fourth of July in his memory. Of course, the row of ice cream freezers still line up on the counter—and we enjoy tasting every flavor.

GRANDPA BAHLER'S HOMEMADE VANILLA ICE CREAM

Yields 1 (6-quart) ice cream canister*

6 eggs, or 1¼ cups pasteurized liquid egg

3¾ cups sugar

¾ teaspoon salt

1 tablespoon vanilla extract (I like to add a tad bit more!)

6 cups half-and-half

6 to 8 cups whole milk

1. In a large bowl, beat the eggs until creamy. Slowly add the sugar while beating. Add the salt and vanilla. Whisk in half-and-half. Pour this mixture into a 6-quart ice cream canister. Add enough whole milk to fill the canister just over half but no more than two-thirds full.

2. Freeze according to the ice cream manufacturer's instructions. The key is to use plenty of ice cream salt and ice. This mixture may take 45 to 60 minutes to freeze. Remove the dasher from the ice cream canister and enjoy!

****Note:** Electric ice cream canisters can be purchased at most hardware stores or online. We purchased our Immergood 6-quart battery-operated ice cream maker from Summit Valley Fabrics in Apple Creek, Ohio, a shop owned by our Amish friends Ivan and Esther Miller.

HOMEMADE BUTTER PECAN ICE CREAM

Yields 1 (6-quart) ice cream canister

We like to experiment with ice cream flavors, and this one ranks at the top of our list of favorites.

1. *To make Roasted Butter Pecans:* Preheat the oven to 350°F. Combine the melted butter, chopped pecans, granulated sugar, and salt. Spread onto a baking sheet. Roast at 350°F for 15 minutes, stirring occasionally. Watch closely so they don't burn. Remove from the oven and set aside to cool.

2. *To make ice cream:* In a pot on the stovetop, combine the brown sugar, granulated sugar, cornstarch, beaten eggs, and pancake syrup. Whisk together and heat, stirring constantly with a flat spatula over medium heat so it doesn't scorch. Gradually add the milk and continue to cook until it thickens. When it thickens, remove from heat and stir in the roasted pecans, heavy cream, and vanilla.

3. Pour the mixture into a 6-quart ice cream freezer and freeze according to the manufacturer's instructions. Use plenty of ice and salt. Remove the dasher and put the lid back on. Pack with more salt and ice if needed. This ice cream is best if allowed to "ripen" for a couple of hours before serving.

Roasted Butter Pecans

3 tablespoons butter, melted

¾ cup chopped pecans

1 tablespoon granulated sugar

⅛ teaspoon salt

For ice cream

½ cup packed brown sugar

¼ cup granulated sugar

2 tablespoons cornstarch or Thermflo

2 eggs, beaten

⅓ cup maple-flavored pancake syrup

3½ cups milk

1½ cups heavy cream

1 tablespoon vanilla extract

CRUMBS FROM *the Table*

Here are a few random tips, ideas, and suggestions from my kitchen. Some are strictly preferential, and some are things I have found to be helpful along the way.

- Always use real butter. Never substitute with margarine or butter blend. Results will not be the same.

- Dark nonstick baking pans tend to make the finished product appear dark and burnt.

- When baking in a glass pan, decrease the temperature 25°F below what the recipe suggests.

- For the best results, always use 2% or whole milk for baking and cooking.

- When melting chocolate in the microwave, heat low (50 percent power) and slow. This will prevent the chocolate from "seizing," or clumping. Stopping frequently and stirring thoroughly helps melt the chocolate and keeps it from overheating.

- For soft chewy cookies, do not overbake.

- To keep cookies as fresh as possible, store them in an airtight container in the freezer as soon as they are baked. When you need to take cookies to an event or to serve them to guests, remove them from the freezer about an hour before serving.

- When measuring brown sugar, always pack it in the measuring cup.

- Never pack flour when measuring.

- When a recipe calls for mayonnaise, I recommend Hellman's. There are certain brands that I tend to use, such as Velveeta and Crisco. In the recipes, these are usually referred to generically—as process cheese spread and solid vegetable shortening, for example. That way you can choose accordingly. Other times I list a specific brand, but don't hesitate to use a brand or substitute you prefer.

- Use real vanilla extract instead of imitation vanilla.

- When working in the kitchen, wash dishes as you work to prevent a backlog of dirty dishes.

- When serving sour cream as a topping (such as on a taco bar), or as a topping for chili, thin down the sour cream with a little water. It doesn't take much, but it takes the thick "glop" out of the sour cream and makes it much easier to dip into and spread. It does not change the flavor.

- When recipes call for onion, I use white or yellow, unless specified otherwise.

- Purchase minced garlic in a jar to use in recipes. It is a time-saver.

- Purchase a kitchen scale to keep in your kitchen. I am amazed how many times I use this tool.

- Shipshewana Happy Salt is an ingredient you will see listed in many of my recipes. This is an all-purpose seasoning that we sell at The Homestead. We use it in our Homestead production recipes, and it is a staple in my own kitchen cupboard. It may be substituted with your favorite seasoning or purchased at The Homestead or online.

- Thermflo is also listed in multiple recipes. This ingredient, which can be used interchangeably with flour, cornstarch, or Clear Jel, can be found in most bulk food stores. I prefer to use Thermflo in my kitchen. It has exceptional heat and cold tolerance for thickening a wide range of foods. It is derived from waxy maize and does not contain wheat gluten, so it is considered gluten free.

- For minimal mess, fry your bacon in a 400°F oven for 10 to 20 minutes, or until it is as crispy as you'd like.

- Save bacon grease or drippings in a container in the refrigerator. Dip into the solidified grease with a spoon and heat in the skillet when making scrambled eggs. It adds so much flavor!

- A bag of frozen peas makes a wonderful ice pack. It can be frozen and reused. I suggest marking the bag so you know to use this only as an ice pack and not for cooking.

- To soften a stick of butter in the microwave, leave it in the paper wrap and microwave it for 4 to 5 seconds, then rotate to another side and repeat. Continue to repeat until the butter is softened but not melted.

TEN WAYS TO

Serve Others

THROUGH FOOD AND HOSPITALITY

1. Take a meal to a family with a new baby or someone in need.

2. Organize a meal train on Perfect Potluck or any other free online tool for coordinating meals.

3. Volunteer to cook or bring food to church events.

4. Serve at a food drive or a soup kitchen.

5. Go the extra mile by adding special touches, such as delivering a fresh bouquet of flowers along with a gifted meal. Include a card with a gift certificate to your favorite shop.

6. If you share a home with others, make your spouse or roommate their favorite cup of morning coffee.

7. Offer to bake for charity bake sales.

8. Get a group of friends together and create meal kits for people from the church or community who are housebound.

9. Let your family decide their meal for their birthday! Make it for them, then surprise them with their favorite cake and a gift card to their favorite coffee shop.

10. Create a calendar at work for employees to sign up for Snack Day. On Snack Day, everyone can bring in their favorite snack to share with coworkers on their breaks. Don't forget to include the recipe!

"For I was an hungred, and ye gave me meat: I was thirsty, and ye gave me drink:
I was a stranger, and ye took me in." —Matthew 25:35

HOW TO HOST
Dinner Guests

For as far back as I can remember, my mom and dad always opened their home in service to others. I wish I could count the guests who have been seated around their table! My parents are truly an example of what Christ teaches: "And whatsoever ye do, do it heartily, as to the Lord, and not unto men" (Colossians 3:23). Mom taught me a lot about hosting. She always made it seem effortless, although I know better. It takes time and energy to host, but the blessings in return are worth the effort.

- Plan your guest list and invite guests into your home with as much notice as possible. However, sometimes it is listening to that last-minute notion of inviting guests that results in the best turnout.

- Hosting company doesn't always mean you need to set the table with good dishes. I like to keep a good supply of paper products ready, and I keep a caddy for plastic cutlery always stocked. The time spent with my guests, family, and grandchildren is far more important than time spent working at the kitchen sink.

- Grab seasonal napkins when you find them, especially after the changing seasons, when you can often find them on sale and stock up.

- Plan your menu and let guests bring a dish if they offer. In our church fellowship, it is common to ask what we can bring for the meal when we receive an invitation.

- Work ahead with food preparation, doing as much beforehand as possible. This is where I learned to use the freezer in my favor. Most dishes can be prepped ahead, frozen, then thawed and baked on the day that guests arrive. This greatly reduces the stress level in the kitchen.

- Do your cleaning a couple of days ahead. This includes cleaning out the refrigerator. There is nothing worse than trying to find room in the refrigerator when you have guests.

- Light candles around your home for a welcoming vibe as guests enter. Nothing says welcome like the warmth and light of candle glow.

- Walk around your garden or yard—or even the roadside ditch—and cut some fresh flowers to display on the table. Or ask your neighbors for some cuttings.

- Have all your dishes washed up and the counters clear when guests arrive.

- Play soft instrumental background music as guests arrive and during dinner.

- When clearing the food after the meal, portion any leftovers and freeze to be pulled out on a busy workday.

- Lead the flow of the time together. Have some conversation ideas in mind.

- Always put salt and pepper out on the table. Even if you don't think it is necessary, it is courteous.

- Do a final cleanup before you go to bed. When my siblings and I were growing up, after guests left, Mom would set the timer for a five-minute cleanup. Everyone pitched in, and it was a fun challenge to see how fast we could work to get the house back in shape.

- Take time to reflect on the beauty of the time together and the blessings you've received by hosting.

"It is more blessed to give than to receive." —Acts 20:35

About
THE HOMESTEAD

I sn't it interesting to look back and see the journey of our lives? If I were to look at my family's in storybook picture form, I would not see a straight, smooth path. I would see twists, turns, bumps, dips, peaks, valleys, and even a few smooth spots. A few storm clouds, a few tears mingled with the sun. Through it all, I would see God's sovereignty, grace, and wisdom. And so it continues . . . this thing called life. We are thankful that God's mercies are new every morning. We rise, and we continue to do the things that God has called us to do.

In May 2008, Mike and I experienced the complete loss of our old home on the farm to fire. In a split second, our earthly possessions became just "things and stuff." Gone. But we *had it all.* Our five precious girls, ages eleven, ten, ten, seven, and five; each other; a host of family and friends; our surrounding community; and a loving church family that carried us through. We chose not to dwell on the here and now. We rolled up our sleeves and began rebuilding our lives. In March 2009, we were so glad to move *home.* Home to a new dwelling where new memories were anticipated. Mike farmed, and I enjoyed my job as the school nurse in our local community.

November 2009 brought an opportunity to consider opening a small shop in Remington, Indiana. We partnered with Mike's brother and sister-in-law Jeff and Heidi along with our combined twelve children, and we diligently went to work remodeling the storefront in Remington that is known today as The Homestead. On May 10, 2010, we nervously flipped the shingle to open! Our girls all worked there—even the littles donned tiny aprons and pulled a stool up to the dishwasher.

Our business model was designed with several facets in mind. I loved to cook and bake, and Heidi took interest in stocking our store with Amish-style bulk foods—dry and canned goods, baking ingredients, candies, gummies, chocolates, dip mixes, and more. We filled the store with retail gifts, fresh fudge, and freezers that lined the wall. I followed my mom's leading to prepare foods ahead and freeze for customers to purchase and enjoy. We catered meals to local businesses and turned freshly sliced meats and cheeses into toasted sandwiches. Today, our customers enjoy all of this and more. We eventually added a fresh salad bar, homemade soup, and a variety of desserts to our lunch menu.

The first Homestead logo was the depiction of a little red saltbox house, and our business was named The Homestead Buttery & Bakery. We were often asked what *buttery* meant. In early colonial days, a buttery was a room like today's pantry, where dry goods and bottles were stored. Our logo eventually evolved into a sketch, designed by our daughter Larissa, of our new home, which is meaningful and intertwines into our personal story. Our business became commonly known as The Homestead.

The years have brought growth and many, many changes, far too numerous to mention. We opened a second Homestead location in West Lafayette, Indiana, in October 2017. This location sits near Purdue campus, where Boilermakers of all ages frequent our store.

Production grew from the first small kitchen where I hand-rolled pie crusts and made a few casseroles. The first casserole produced was our Chicken and Rice Casserole. It's still one of our top sellers! We take pride in knowing that our products are handmade without added preservatives or fillers. Our foil casserole pans are all microwave safe, which allows customers the ease of quick thawing and baking, even when crunched for time. I still enjoy getting my hands in the dough to roll out loaves of bread. I love the privilege of experimenting with and creating new recipes.

We journeyed on through several changes, locations, and remodels. Today, our production facility operates at an offsite location in Remington where all our frozen products are made and stored to be shipped to our retail stores, online customers, and wholesale customers.

It has been a journey of love and passion for what we do. Our girls are all grown, but we have worked hard together and have created many memories. Our local daughters continue to be involved day to day. We still love to work together hand-decorating thousands of frosted sugar cookies! The girls' tiny Homestead aprons now hang in our play kitchen at home for the grandchildren to enjoy as they whip up their own imaginary meals. May they know the joy of serving others, as Christ taught us to do.

This is a shortened glimpse of our Homestead journey. It's been an honor to serve each of our customers and to work alongside our faithful employees.

Visit us online at www.HomesteadButtery.com,
and please stop and visit our stores when you are in the area!

The Remington Homestead

The West Lafayette Homestead

ACKNOWLEDGMENTS

I am convinced that this dream of mine to publish a cookbook would never have become a reality without the encouragement and support of my dearest people.

My thanks and deepest appreciation to our five daughters: Amber, Larissa, Leandra, Kenzie, and Erin. Without your encouragement to do this sooner than later, we might still be waiting! Larissa and Leandra, your photography styling and skill amazes me, and I am so thankful for your keen eye and clean style. To Amber, Kenzie, and Erin, the workforce behind the scenes: I could not have done this without your part. Who knew that we could create dirty dishes so fast? The hours you spent cleaning up behind me so I could keep making dishes, the clean towels and laundry that continually appeared in the drawers, caring for the littles, and wiping sticky fingers so the mommies could continue to take photos, chopping veggies, cutting garnishes, sweeping the floor, hauling out the trash, picking up the toys . . . the list goes on!

To my best friend and husband, Mike. You are the wind beneath my wings. I adore your quiet wisdom and ability to fix just about anything. I can think of countless evenings that you scrounged around in the refrigerator for something to eat while I pushed through working on this cookbook . . . always without complaint. I am thankful to walk this life with you.

To my five sons-in-law, Thomas, Eli, Kevin, Trenton, and David. I love you like my own. You so graciously supported my dream by sharing your wives and children for days upon days so we could all be together in the kitchen. Thank you for being my taste testers!

To our six precious grandchildren, Jude, Alaya, Lincoln, Addison, Ava, and Caroline. You may not remember the piles of dishes, but I hope you remember the snuggles and bedtime stories. You fill my heart with joy. May you (and future grandbabies, Lord willing) treasure the simple joys of life.

I want to thank my mom, Jane, for teaching me what true love and hospitality mean. Many of the recipes in this book were hand-picked from her own recipe box. I love you, Mom.

On those long days of cooking, baking, and taking photos, we will be forever grateful to Erica, Julia, Hannah, Naomi, and Stacy, who lovingly watched over and cared for our little people so we could work without interruption! They loved you!

To Rachel and Heidi, for your time spent over the kitchen sink washing dishes. You blessed the day.

Tami and Michael, thank you for lending your kitchen for a fun day of photography in its beautiful, natural light. Thanks to Eli and Kenzie, who hit the road and made connections early that morning for props that I left behind at home!

Thank you to my Homestead family. You work hard and treat me well. You have been an encouragement to me throughout the writing process and have been willing to pick up the slack when you knew I was on a time crunch. We are on this journey together.

I am humbled, and thankful to God, my creator, for His eternal gift of salvation. He is the one who knows me best. It is only by His abundant grace that I can live, love, and serve. To God be all glory, forever and ever. Amen.

— Jody

INDEX

THE AUTHOR

Jody Bahler is founder and owner of The Homestead, a specialty home-style bakery, deli, and gift shop where she creates, tests, and tries every recipe. Family-owned by Jody and her husband Mike since 2010, The Homestead, a destination sought by many travelers, has grown to two locations. Jody and her husband have raised five daughters on their five-generational family farmstead in rural Indiana.